ACKNOWLEDGEMENTS

From beginning to end of this project, US style 'Welfare Reform' has gathered momentum so that it is now widely debated and almost daily reported in the media.

We have read numerous state and national reports and wish to thank Boyd Koehler, Augsburg College Library, for his help in keeping us abreast of the plethora of materials and for his constant encouragement. At times the project seemed to unfold too slowly and we are very glad of the critique and creative energy of our writers' group colleagues, Maura Sullivan, Kim Strom-Gottfried, Ron Rooney; also we appreciate colleagues, Mark Peterson, Deborah Lyttelton, Pascale Vassie and Mark Greenberg for their reading of early and later drafts. Nils Dybvig helped to illustrate the reality of lone parents re-entering the workforce in his recipient profiles and we thank him for his continuing work.

We wish to thank Mrs Gwendoline Flatt for her help in scanning the UK press and keeping us in tune with developments by sending clippings from the reaches of Somerset to Minneapolis. Also, thank you to Doran Edwards who helped generate the list of web sites in the appendix. At times our printers jammed, our scanner wouldn't work or our faxes ran out of ink and Kelly Anders, Department Secretary, has been ever helpful in tackling these obstacles. Lastly, we thank our families for their commitment to this work as demonstrated in their support of us and willingness to make supper.

Rosemary Link and Tony Bibus.

This book is dedicated to the memory of
Josephine Melanie MacRae

'Oh, dear me, the world is ill-divided –
Them that works the hardest are the least provided.'

From the 'Jute Mill Song' by Mary Brookbank, Dundee, Scotland, 1920

'*De la esfinge a la caja de caudales hay un hilo tenso
que atraviesa el corazón de todos los niños pobres.*'

'There is a wire stretched from the Sphinx to the safety
deposit box that passes through the heart of all poor children.'

From *Dance of Death* by Federico García Lorca, December, 1929
Translation by Robert Bly in *Lorca and Jiménenez,*
Beacon Press, Boston, 1997, pp. 152-153.

When children pay

US welfare reform and its implications for UK policy

Rosemary J Link and Anthony Bibus with Karen Lyons

Foreword by David Bull

CPAG • 94 White Lion Street • London N1 9PF

CPAG promotes action for the relief, directly or indirectly, of poverty among children and families with children. We work to ensure that those on low incomes get their full entitlements to welfare benefits. In our campaigning and information work we seek to improve benefits and policies for low income families, in order to eradicate the injustice of poverty. If you are not already supporting us, please consider making a donation, or ask for details of our membership schemes and publications.

Poverty Publication 101

Published by CPAG
94 White Lion Street, London N1 9PF

© CPAG 2000

ISBN 1-901698-15-7

The views expressed in this book are the authors' and contributors' and do not necessarily express those of CPAG.

A CIP record for this book is available from the British Library

Typeset by: Boldface, London EC1
Printed by: William Clowes, Beccles, Suffolk

CONTENTS

ABOUT THE CONTRIBUTORS

Anthony Bibus is the BSW programme director and teaches social work at Augsburg College in Minneapolis, Minnesota, USA. He has been a social worker for over 25 years, in child protective services dealing on a daily basis with issues of poverty. Since receiving his doctorate in social work from the Universitiy of Minnesota in 1992, he has been focusing on social policy analysis and on how much social workers can learn from each other worldwide. Dr Bibus is consulting editor for the *Journal of Baccalaureate Social Work* and *Community Alternatives International Journal of Family Care.*

Rosemary Link is professor of social work and Chair, Professional Studies Division, Augsburg College, Minnesota. Dr Link is a former education welfare officer and school social worker in North London, England and has her postgraduate CQSW from Bedford College, London University and her doctorate from the University of Minnesota. She has special interest in international social work, children's issues and family participation in service planning, and has published in these areas. She has led courses for US students on reciprocal exchanges with Slovenia, Mexico and the UK and is an external examiner for the University of the West Indies, Jamaica.

Karen Lyons is reader in social work at the University of East London. Dr Lyons has substantial experience in the field of European exchange schemes and has run a degree programme in international social work studies since 1994. Her research interests include educational and career patterns of social workers as well as comparative and international social work. The last area is reflected in a recently published text *International Social Work: Themes and Perspectives.*

David Bull is associate senior lecturer in international social welfare and public policy at the University of Bristol, in which capacity he directs credit-earning programmes for Americans. He has held five visiting positions in North American universities, most recently as Professor of International Affairs at East Carolina University. He was a member from 1967–97 of CPAG's Executive Committee, which he chaired from 1989–93.

PREFACE

This book is directly concerned with children in poverty. We examine the current social welfare policies in the US and the UK that have tried and often failed to meet children's needs, and we explore alternative solutions for the new century, especially for UK policy-makers. There is an urgent need for this policy analysis at a time when people in many European countries are listening intently to US governors such as Tommy Thompson in Wisconsin, who encourages the perception that reduction of welfare rolls means reduction of poverty.

European policies have been CPAG's chief source for international comparative analysis until recently when the claimed 'successes' of US politicians drew the attention of the current Labour Government. In view of the renewed interest in US welfare legislation, this book seeks to scrutinize the impact of 'welfare reform'. Such scrutiny is especially crucial to prevent uncritically importing policies from countries where the unequal distribution of wealth, which is well documented for the 1980s and 90s in the US, threatens the well-being of many children. Also, as we enter the millennium it is timely to recommit to ending child poverty. One hundred years ago, Lloyd George introduced a 'War Budget', not to make war in Europe, but to wage war on poverty. Ironically, exactly a century later, New Labour has announced its own renewed attention to child poverty and the dialogue is not different enough considering the time that has elapsed.

There have been stunning advances on many fronts during the last century, but alleviating child poverty has not been one of them. As the world becomes more accessible, CPAG looks to the experience of others to learn, to challenge and to seek more powerful tools to achieve children's well-being. There is currently a much touted policy of 'Welfare Reform' in the US, a policy which aims to save taxpayers money and to make people independent. This book rejects the conflation of dependency with poverty. We are all to some degree dependent on others. Many people living in poverty are demonstrating immense creativity in surviving and are role models of resilience as they raise their children. While some innovations can stimulate new thinking about poverty, the focus on punishment in the form of 'sanctions' is one example of policy which is totally wrong for the UK. The following pages lay out some of the issues and potential learning from a review of US policy and its applicability to current policy planning in the UK.

On a personal note, as an Education Welfare Officer in Camden in the 1970s, I (Link) visited a great many homes on the housing estates of Kentish Town and Euston. There are children in my mind's eye who experienced absolute poverty – not enough to eat, overcrowded housing, lack of heat, inadequate clothing, persistent respiratory illnesses. Some of them endured with particular resilience and this book acknowledges them and the lessons they taught me about people's capacities when faced with constant challenge. It is our hope that we can be part of a society that ensures that their children have different futures.

Rosemary Link and Anthony Bibus.

FOREWORD

DAVID BULL, CPAG EXECUTIVE COMMITTEE MEMBERS (1967–97)

This is not the first time we, at CPAG, have found ourselves debating the arrival from America of a welfare-something-or-another.

Thirty years ago, we were talking 'welfare rights'. Now, 'welfare reform' is all the rage. But what does it mean for the UK to import the notion of welfare – with whatever suffix – when the word has such a different meaning in the USA?

I raise that question from the perspective of having served on CPAG's first welfare rights stall in 1968 and of having reflected often since then, with both British and American students, on the perpetual problems of US welfare. So I am pleased to have been given the space in this foreword not just to extend an enthusiastic welcome to a well-researched book warning us against thoughtlessly importing 'welfare reform', but to unpack both of these words. If we are to address the muddle and confusion that exists in this regard we need to ask ourselves three questions:

- how is the word 'welfare' being used here;
- which kinds of 'reform' seem to be at issue; *and*
- in so far as these reforms are of American origin, what questions are raised for us, in the chapters that follow, as to the challenges and dilemmas of transposing any of those reforms into British politics, policy and practice?

THE LANGUAGE OF 'WELFARE'

It used to be so simple. The British – in common with their European neighbours – had something they called a 'welfare state'. It referred not only to income maintenance – the generic term used in this book to embrace both means-tested ('assistance') benefits and non means-tested (mostly 'insurance'-based) support – but also, we all more or less agreed, to at least four other social services: housing; health care; education; and personal social services.

We might use inverted commas, in anticipation of quibbles as to the boundaries of this 'welfare state', but there appeared to be consensus enough that it signalled a comprehensive provision – the more so, of course, if we endorsed the Titmussian notion[1] that two additional forms of welfare were available to some through taxation and the workplace.

True, welfare did have another, less embracing, meaning. At the local level of personal social service delivery, we had Welfare Departments; and Karen Lyons recalls how front-line workers in other services were also perceived as 'the welfare'. Although this might mean that the narrow, departmental meaning could detract from the wider concept,[2] it seemed legitimate, nevertheless, to talk of welfare both generically and in a particular area of service provision.

Americans, meanwhile, were using the term to refer to the public assistance benefits discussed in Chapter 2 below. They might refer to 'social welfare' when they wanted to embrace other benefits and services of what we would call a 'welfare state', but their welfare, plain and simple, was what we called 'assistance'. And that was the sense in which we carelessly adopted, in the late 1960s, the language of 'welfare rights'. When I say 'we', I include myself[3] among those who followed Tony Lynes[4] down the road of using an American term as if it made sense in a British context.

The National Welfare Rights Organisation (NWRO) had been established, in the USA of the 1960s, to campaign for 'More Money Now!'.[5] The 'welfare rights' being asserted by the NWRO were to entitlements set out in the regulations at state level – New York was the leading case – to public assistance. In a word, welfare. If we were to assert similar rights in the UK – leaving aside for the moment the matter of there being few rights in the discretion-dominated, regulation-free system – then it made little sense to call them welfare.

But welfare rights was a catchy slogan and it caught on. Coincidentally, 'Welfare Departments' were abolished in the Seebohm reforms of the 1970s. It was as if we suddenly substituted a new narrow meaning for welfare. Pretty soon, CPAG was deciding to follow the NWRO example of publishing a guide to this kind of welfare. If they were subject to unregulated discretion, then we could hardly call them rights. So, starting in 1969, the Group published what soon became its annual *National Welfare Benefits Handbook* – as distinct from a parallel series of guides to contributory (and other non means-tested) benefits as of right.

True, these two guide books have of late become one – with a CD-rom version for good measure – and the *Welfare Benefits Handbook* now covers both means-tested and non-means-tested benefits. But this reflects a publishing decision about the best way CPAG could get its guides to its users. It in no way detracts from the distinction between universal and selective benefits that remains as fundamental to CPAG's position as it always was. Aneurin Bevan's boast, of 1948, that assistance would 'wither away' was never realised, although both major parties pretended, to differing degrees over the next 30 years, that it remained an objective – if not achievable by improving the provisions of social insurance, then perhaps by amalgamating the tax system with benefits in some form of 'negative income tax' or by extending work-based pensions (thus extending the coverage of Titmuss's other 'welfare states').

What nobody seemed yet to be suggesting was that assistance benefits might be reduced – or at least withdrawn from certain categories of claimant. Except, of course, from the workshy and the fraudulent. If the age-old witch-hunt to deny benefits to the 'sturdy beggar' had never gone away,[6] the British were not yet in the business – long-established in Southern states of the USA especially – of 'periodic campaigns' to invent and enforce rules that would 'purge the rolls'.[7]

Then, the more you studied America's welfare, the more regularly you would read of 'welfare reform', almost as if the two words had become one. It seemed to be something US politicians could repeatedly promise as if previous failures could not possibly indicate that there were serious obstacles to reform. When, I wondered, had these promises begun?

REFORMING WHOSE WELFARE?

That question took me back to 1971. That was when Piven and Cloward introduced us to the practice of 'purging the rolls'. And it was the year in which the journal, *Current History*, produced a special issue on 'Welfare', with a lead article by the doyen of American income maintenance, Wilbur Cohen, on 'welfare reform'.[8] Cohen declared his goal of 'true welfare reform'. It may have 'marked a basic departure', for him, when the USA eventually introduced European-style insurance rights in 1935, but a 'true' reform would put an end to means-testing.

By 1971, of course, there were those, on either side of the Atlantic, who were envisaging that this end could best be achieved not by improving the protection of insurance but, as I have intimated, by some form of negative income tax. While Cohen opted for a structural solution, he was concerned to avoid the alternatives of what we might call 'urging' or 'purging' that were being championed by those American reformers for whom the receipt of welfare indicated individual fallibility. In the first of these options, new incentives must be found to persuade recipients to leave welfare for what would increasingly be called 'workfare.' If those inducements failed, then the rolls would have to be 'purged' in some other way.

It was this notion of 'purging' that forcibly struck me – initially upon reading Piven and Cloward in 1971 and then from my first sight of American welfare in action in 1977 – as a feature that especially distinguished the American approach from the British way of doing things. Give or take the spasmodic witch-hunts of the workshy or the anti-fraud campaigns of various kinds, with which CPAG was very soon concerned,[9] the British focus was more clearly fixed on the 'true welfare reform' that had attracted Cohen. If there were too many Britons on assistance, this represented a failure not of poor people, but of social insurance (or, for some dreamers, a failure to 'simplify' by somehow combining tax and benefit systems).

The notion that the British rolls might likewise be purged has not appeared suddenly on the Blair Agenda. The Americanization of the British approach to assistance has been more insidious than that. Without attempting to trace that process step-by-step, we might venture back to 1954, when the Phillips Committee reported on the first 'crisis' in post war income maintenance. That Committee was concerned with the basic paradox that was by then presenting itself in the claiming behaviour of retired people. On the one hand, too many were applying for National Assistance: this was not the residual benefit that Aneurin Bevan had envisaged. Yet it could also be said that too few were applying: of those eligible for this not-so-residual benefit, too many were reluctant to claim (for reasons that were to be elucidated in other reports that followed in the 1960s[10] and which were to become a feature of a European concern with 'take-up' – an issue that receives so little attention in the USA).

The Phillips Committee essentially advocated a two-pronged policy: keep down the numbers on assistance, by improving the coverage of insurance; but accept also that something needed to be done to improve the image of assistance.[11] Both major political parties knew what they wanted to do in the first regard: introduce graduated pensions – and, subsequently, graduated benefits for other categories of claimant. The image-changing took a little longer; but eventually, after further investigation into the nature and extent of the assistance deterrent, the Ministry of Social Security Act 1966 introduced some of the cosmetic changes that would allegedly make it less stigmatic to 'claim' (no longer 'apply for') assistance benefits.[12]

It will be noticed that, 20 years after the Assistance and Insurance legislation of 1946-48, the focus was largely on one claimant group: pensioners. Predominantly female, of course. And white. This was very different from the American emphasis. The concern there was also with women, but they were young lone parents and disproportionately black (of which more in Chapter 3). It cannot be stressed too strongly that the first 15 to 20 years of the UK's post war debate on poverty and income maintenance – until a 'rediscovery of poverty' in 1965 that was essentially about child poverty – concerned older people.[13] The USA was a much younger population and a generation behind the UK in contemplating the 'burden' of old age.

Eventually, the cross-party pretence, among British politicians, that they would somehow restore assistance to its 'safety net' role exposed by civil servants for what it was. Their *Social Assistance* report of 1978 – commissioned by a Labour Government worried about the growth in public expenditure generally and of the demand-led benefits budget in particular[14] – made it plain: governments would not find the money to spend on the universalist programmes that would keep the assistance rolls to the size envisaged 30 years earlier; we should stop pretending that assistance would ever play that residual role and accept that it was now playing a 'mass role.' In order that this role might be affordable social assistance needed, the civil servants reasoned, to shed some of its more expensive habits: let local government attend to the rents of poor tenants; while labour-intensive discretion should be replaced by the kind of 'itemized' entitlements that American welfare rights activists had vigorously pursued.[15]

This Americanization was ironic in that the leading British expert (the UK's Cohen-equivalent and the only authority acknowledged in *Social Assistance*) had warned against such a legalistic approach to discretionary extras.[16] But down that road the incoming Thatcher Government eagerly skeltered, rushing through under-refined regulations.[17]

This 'reform' was short-lived. Too many wretched people claimed their legalized entitlements[18] and new rationing devices had to be found in the 1986 Act. By now, the Thatcher and Reagan administrations had each come to appreciate two 'rules' of income maintenance expenditure. For a start, if you want to target benefits by resorting to more means-testing, then the biggest pot to aim at is the payment of universalist retirement pensions. On the other hand, though, no Conservative or Republican government is that keen to alienate its older electorate. Plenty of these voters may want cuts in income maintenance, but not in their chunk of it.

The grey vote was common cause in both countries. If you promise cuts in income maintenance budgets but retirement pensions are sacrosanct, then you are going to have to find a more vulnerable target. If, as I have been suggesting, this was familiar territory for American reformers, it was new ground for British politicians. To assist them in this journey, these policy-makers adopted another weapon from the US: a new terminology for blaming the victim. Charles Murray was the flavour of the decade and the mantra of the 'dependency culture' was catching on.[19] Benefits were to blame for people's poverty: so cut them to enable these people to escape poverty. As this creed began to be put into practice in several states of the USA (described in Chapters 1–3) the Conservative admirers in the UK of this American way were losing office to New Labour.

The enthusiasm for welfare reform was not, however, lost. Tony Blair even appointed a Minister for Welfare Reform. And the Wisconsin reformers came to London in various guises.[20] It would have been hard enough to assess where any of this might be heading, without the confusion of language. What was the British reader to make of a politician's statement of intent that used the word welfare to mean two or three different things? Robert Walker has blamed this tendency on the recruitment to Downing Street of US educated and influenced policy advisers and to a desire to find an alliteration with 'workfare'.[21]

Maybe so – although Frank Field, the former CPAG Director who was to become the aforesaid Minister for Welfare Reform, has surely made a considerable contribution, starting in Opposition, to this terminological waywardness. The reader soon discovers that the 'welfare' referred to in the title of his 1995 book[22] was neither welfare in the strict American sense nor welfare as in a 'welfare state'. For Field, a welfare state was a synonym for the income maintenance system, in which there was both 'insurance-based welfare' and 'means-tested welfare'. And Field wanted to see the former improved to rid the welfare state of the poison of the latter – an objective loyal to his CPAG past; but wherever had he acquired such a vocabulary?

His various forms of welfare were never defined: you had to adjust to the novelty of the usage as you went along. That might not matter a great deal to many observers of the recent British debate. Like the authors of this book, though, I am less sanguine. If we are to understand the parameters of 'welfare reform' – whether as citizens being promised legislative change or as anti-poverty campaigners seeking to engage in a responsible debate – then unambiguous definitions do matter. Yet, confused usage has become epidemic. When Frank Field became the Minister for Welfare Reform, he continued to confuse the issue. And, we shall see, his Westminster colleagues, including the Prime Minister, have tended to be just as haphazard.

The more is the pity, since Field, the Minister, was soon contributing a fine point of language to this welfare debate. Taking up his Government's promise of radical welfare reform,[23] he reasoned that, literally speaking, this meant that any changes should start from the roots, taking into account the values and culture that have shaped what is to be reformed. If we accept that premiss, then it surely follows that we should be wary of uprooting, from their own cultural history, the ideas and practices of other countries – which means, in the instant case, the United States of America.

WHAT CAN BE TRANSFERRED?

Mr Blair and his Social Security ministers will be less likely to make that mistake if they heed the above warning from his first Minister for Welfare Reform. This book amply augments that advice (witness the recommendations in Chapter 5) with evidence from America – although the Government has already had available to it other warnings derived both from what has happened in the USA and from an awareness of why some of those occurrences are unlikely to be transferable. I shall draw here upon two such sources: a symposium where Frank Field debated 'Lessons from America' with Lawrence Mead, a prominent American thinker on this subject;[24] and the report, from the Social Security Select Committee, on a visit to the USA, notably to the model state of Wisconsin.[25]

From these two reports, we can glean two checklists: one of American approaches that could be replicated in the UK; the other of Anglo-American differences that will stand more steadfastly in the way of such imports.

The Social Security Committee was concerned that a fundamental difference – between the federal USA and the unitary UK – should not be used as an excuse for saying that the British are less able than the Americans to experiment. Of course, the freedom of American states to do their own thing in many aspects of welfare administration means that they can learn from each other's trials and errors. Driven by the populist imperative to 'get welfare out of Washington',[26] the states may effectively be conducting experiments whether they intend to or not. But that advantage of a federal system should not be used as an excuse, the Social Security Committee reasoned, to avoid pilot projects in selected areas of the UK.[27]

That plea sits well with Frank Field's crusade for more local autonomy in benefit offices.[28] On average, Field has calculated, staff in area and local offices pay out £1m per employee per year and should have more say in the administration of those payments.[29] Any such change will need to be accompanied – and the Select Committee agrees – by a change in 'bureaucratic culture'.[30] Mead takes this as axiomatic, apparently feeling no more need than the Committee to offer any evidence of what this would involve, let alone how it was to be achieved. Whatever it may have taken in Wisconsin and elsewhere in the USA, nobody seems to be insinuating that British officials are inherently and irrevocably more resistant to change than their American counterparts. The British literature on benefit administration, developing from 1970s,[31] may suggest that office customs could be a serious obstacle. I might have been more convinced of this had I not witnessed, at close quarters, the remarkable change – seemingly at the flick of a training session or two – in the behaviour of the presenting officer at Social Security Appeal hearings, from vindictive adversary to helpful *amicus curiae*.

But, if the bureaucratic culture is susceptible to change, how much more resistant might the popular culture be? We know, from endless polls, that public opinion can be extremely volatile. That does not tell us much, though, about what kind of articulate and influential majority might rally behind any particular aspect of US 'reform' that a British Government might propose to replicate. If we take the levels of demonstrations in Westminster – whether in the voting lobbies or on the pavements – as a guide to public concern, then it might be concluded that the Government is as free as ever to mess unemployed people around but that it may have over-estimated the willingness of the allegedly put-upon taxpayer to support sanctions on lone mothers and people with disabilities. As the Select Committee warned, any British consensus for change may be for one that entails taking fewer risks and creating fewer casualties than the American consensus has seemed willing to tolerate.[32]

Furthermore even if, as this book reminds us, Americans have been willing to punish 'welfare moms', will they continue to support sanctions against mothers once they appreciate that the victims are their children? If the sanctions are what the American electorate is believed to have voted for, then how 'horrified', asks the President of Bread for the World (quoted in Chapter 5) will 'decent people' be when they see the outcome?

And what of decent people in the UK? How far down the less liberal US road, the authors ask, might they be prepared to go? The Westminster rebellions may give us a clue, especially when coupled with the expression of concern, by the Social Security Committee, about the 'potentially damaging' effects of the Wisconsin policy, whereby lone mothers are deemed eligible to restart work once their youngest child is 12 weeks old.[33] But, then, as Chapter 3 reminds us, British means-tested benefits have never been focused on lone parenthood in the way that American welfare has been. Noting this difference,[34] the Select Committee cites other clients – those who are unemployed or disabled – with which British reform will be necessarily concerned. Whichever client-group is being targeted, however, there is a common underlying theme: how much sooner might its members be dispatched back to the labour market? The British obstacles may be not only cultural but institutional.

In the former regard, it is not just our more liberal concern to avoid 'casualties'; there is also the question (addressed in Chapter 4) of how ready the British might be to develop an American attitude to life-long learning.[35] However well that point is taken and whatever the willingness of government to invest in programmes that really do re-equip its workless citizens for new opportunities – like those discussed in Chapters 4 and 5 – there remains the obstacle that worried the Select Committee: the British economy does not have the demand for labour that the American economy generates.[36]

The Committee goes on, however, to qualify its own concern: thanks to an overall increase in employment opportunities and to particular shifts – as in the creation both of more temporary jobs and of more flexible work patterns – the UK now has 'the right opportunities to reform its social security system'. That conclusion seems less than self-evident. It is far from obvious how taking a temporary job as an alternative to a weekly guarantee of benefits can be described as 'social security'. And the IEA debaters, regardless of the perspective they were coming from, were far less sanguine about British prospects. For a start, Mead is concerned[37] that, even in the US, part-time jobs are an inadequate solution: full-time, permanent jobs are needed. The Minnesota mantra, quoted in Chapter 2, that 'any job is better than no job' will not wash: how can you enforce sanctions against non-workers, Mead asks,[38] if there is an inadequate supply of suitable jobs?

And we would surely be concerned if and when parents were obliged (as in Chapter 3) to leave welfare for a sub-minimum wage. For Mead, though, the supply of jobs is more important than the problem of low pay – especially if the UK is tackling the latter with a Minimum Wage[39] – although he admits that unattractive pay contributes to the unsteadiness of employment with which he is principally concerned. Whether or not you agree with that appraisal,[40] there would appear to be considerable support for John Philpott's anxiety on behalf of jobless households who are 'excluded from the wider economy and society'.[41] While we may look with him to an improved economy that would offer hope and opportunities to these households, there is surely no gainsaying his conclusion that benefits offer many such Britons more security than work does.

But there's the rub. American 'Social Security' serves deserving groups, while 'welfare' is the residuum for those with a less popular claim upon the public purse. While that same divide – in attitudes if not nomenclature – has long afflicted the British debate, 'social security' has continued to be offered to all manner of citizens who can prove 'need' – no matter that some must jump through tougher hoops than others and expect more limited awards.

Some aspects of that security may have been undermined by successive governments – with the Thatcher administrations sometimes willing to demolish what their Labour predecessors had been content merely to erode – but the Blair Government should mark seriously the cross-party concern, on the back benches, that British voters may be less ready than their American counterparts for an increase in social and economic *in*-security.

NOTES

1 For the classic exposition of how 'fiscal welfare' and 'occupational welfare' favour certain beneficiaries, see R M Titmus, 'The Social Division of Welfare', in *Essays on the 'Welfare State'*, Allen & Unwin, 1958, Ch 2.

2 M Brown, 'A Welfare Service – not a Welfare Department', *Social Service*

Quarterly, Vol. 39, No. 3, 1965, pp91–98 and 112.

3 D Bull, *Action for Welfare Rights*, Fabian Research Series 286, 1970.

4 T Lynes, *Welfare Rights*, Fabian Tract 395, 1970.

5 T Lynes, 'More Money Now!' *Poverty*, No.5, CPAG, 1967, pp6–8.

6 P Golding and S Middleton , *Images of Welfare*, Martin Robertson, 1982.

7 F Fox Piven and R Cloward, *Regulating the Poor: the functions of public welfare*, Pantheon, 1971, Ch 4.

8 W Cohen , 'Welfare Reform: a persistent quest', *Current History*, Vol. 61, No. 363, 1971, pp257–260 and 305.

9 Editorial, 'Where are the Workshy?', *Poverty*, No 9, CPAG, 1968, pp1–4.

10 See especially Ministry of Pensions and National Insurance, *Financial and other circumstances of Retirement Pensioners*, HMSO, 1966.

11 Phillips Committee, *Report of the Committee on the Economic and Financial Problems of the Provision for Old Age*, Cmd. 9333, HMSO, 1954, paras 213–215.

12 A Webb, The Abolition of National Assistance: policy changes in the administration of assistance benefits', in P Hall and others, *Change, Choice and Conflict in Social Policy*, Heinemann, 1975, Ch 14.

13 For the landmark statement of the 'rediscovery', see B Abel-Smith and P Townsend, *The Poor and the Poorest*, Bell 1965. For the consequent shift of emphasis from retirement pensions to family poverty, see, for instance, D Bull, 'The rediscovery of family poverty', in D Bull (ed.), *Family Poverty*, Duckworth, 1971, Ch 1.

14 C Walker, *Managing Poverty: the limits of social assistance*, Routledge, 1993.

15 DHSS, *Social Assistance: a review of the Supplementary Benefits scheme in Great Britain*, HMSO, 1978, paras 1.12 and 1.28–1.29.

16 R M Titmuss, 'Welfare "Rights", Law and Discretion', *Political Quarterly*, Vol. 42, No. 2, 1971, pp113–32.

17 J Allbeson and R Smith, *We don't give Clothing Grants any more: the 1980 Supplementary Benefit scheme*, Poverty Pamphlet 62, 1984, p105.

18 Secretary of State for Social Services, Reform of Social Security, Vol. 1, Cmnd. 9517 and Vol. 2, Cmnd. 9518, 1985.

19 C Murray, *Losing Ground: American social policy 1950–1980*, Basic Books, 1984. For an assessment of the relevance and impact of this concept in the UK, see H Dean and P Taylor-Gooby, *Dependency Culture: the explosion of a myth*, Harvester-Wheatsheaf, 1992.

20 J J Rogers, 'Making welfare work', *New Statesman*, 29 August, 1997. The back cover of that issue of the *New Statesman* announced that Governor Tommy Thompson of Wisconsin would be speaking at the magazine's imminent conference on 'How Labour Can Deliver'.

21 R Walker, 'Counting Time', *SPA News*, October/November, 1999.

22 F Field, *Making Welfare Work: reconstructing welfare for the millennium*, Institute of Community Studies, 1995.

23 F Field, 'Radicalisation and Welfare Reform' (Prospect lecture), 15 December, 1997. reproduced in F Field *Reflections on Welfare Reform*, Social Market Foundation, 1998.

24 A Deacon (ed.) *From Welfare to Work: lessons from America*, Institute of Economic Affairs, 1997.

25 Social Security Committee, *Social Security Reforms: lessons from the United States of America*, HC 552, 1998.

26 L Mead, 'From Welfare to Work: lessons from America', in Deacon (note 24), p47.

27 Social Security Committee (note 25), para 13.

28 F Field, 'Reinventing Welfare: a response to Lawrence Mead', in Deacon (note 24), p63.

29 F Field 'Big Brother is listening to you', (Lloyds-TSB Forum, 27 October, 1997; copy of the presented paper kindly supplied by F Field).

30 Mead (note 26), p44; Field (note 27), p63; Social Security Committee (note 25), para 15.

31 See, notably, M Hill, *The Sociology of Public Administration*, Weidenfeld and Nicolson, 1972, Ch 4; D Donnison, 'Against Discretion', *New Society*, 15 September, 1977, pp534–536.

32 Social Security Committee (note 25), para 6.

33 Social Security Committee (note 25), para 10; see also para 20.

34 Social Security Committee (note 25), para 8.

35 A Grimes, 'Would Workfare Work? – an alternative approach for the UK', in Deacon (note 24), p102.

36 Social Security Committee (note 25), para 20.

37 Mead (note 26), pp3–4 and 7.

38 Mead (note 26), p ix.

39 Mead (note 26), p8.

40 For a contrary view, see D Cook, 'Welfare to Work – and back again?' in Deacon (note 24), p111.

41 J Philpott, 'Lessons from America: workfare and Labour's New Deal', in Deacon (note 24), p67.

Introduction

'I cannot help hoping and believing that before this generation has passed away we shall have advanced a great step towards that good time when poverty, and the wretchedness and human degradation which always follow in its camp, will be as remote to the people of this country as the wolves which once infested its forests.'
                    (Lloyd George, British Chancellor, Budget speech 1909)

People rarely choose to raise children in poverty. Yet, despite recent dramatic prosperity in some countries, poverty exists in all nations and is a persistent drain on the lives of children. In most parts of the world, those who have access to wealth are improving their position, while the number of people living in poverty is increasing.[1] Since this is a global issue, when countries such as the UK seek to reform their approach to poverty and the well-being of families, particularly women and children, they can learn from one another. This book is an examination of the current revisions in US 'welfare' policy, and asks what the UK can learn from both the policy and the implementation process.

In the summer of 1996, President Bill Clinton signed Public Law 104.193, the Personal Responsibility and Work Opportunity Reconciliation Act, effectively ending six decades of welfare as the people of the US had come to know it. No longer would children be entitled to at least a minimum of income support from the federal government. Now the primary responsibility for the welfare of children is 'devolved' or passed down to each of the 50 states, and parents are expected to secure jobs to support their families. No parent can depend on federal government assistance beyond a maximum of 60 months in their life time. The explicit change is from entitlements and safety net to individual *responsibility* and expectation that adults take the *opportunity* to work, regardless of the ages of children in the family. Assistance is temporary and if people do not comply, they face being *sanctioned* (reduction of benefits as penalty for non-compliance). For many children in families experiencing poverty, this means that their families will stop receiving cash welfare grants by the year 2002. The policy changes behind four hundred pages of legislation are summarized in Figure 1.1. The Act has been implemented at varying rates from state to state, according to a state's readiness with plans, evaluation procedures and trial periods. Minnesota and Wisconsin were in the forefront and are discussed in Chapter 2, Alabama and Mississippi were two of the slowest states to prepare, with resulting low take-up of federal matching funds.

This Act, to be referred to as 'Welfare Reform', has established political sucess at a number of levels: moving many people into the workplace, firing politicians with enthusiasm at the 'falling rolls' of adults receiving public assistance, giving welfare workers more responsibility at the local level for dispensing money and interpreting income maintenance guidelines, giving people a sense of change in policy that had languished and needed overhaul. Despite these successes, however, the enduring criticisms of the legislation are many layered and include stark consequences for children in the poorest families. As stated by Robert Greenstein, Director of the Center on Budget Policy and Priorities (CBPP),

> With the lowest unemployment rate in 30 years, we might have expected greater progress in reducing both the number of poor children and the extent of their poverty. Instead, poor children are getting poorer.[2]

The positive economy in the US has benefited most people and in particular the wealthiest Americans; but for those children in families below the poverty line (according to the CBPP, 10.2 million in 1998), the reduction in benefits has produced dire and incompletely recognised, but very real, consequences. As the millennium turns, child poverty in the US and the UK stubbornly persists. The news of recent 'successes' in US welfare reform may induce a sense of ready transferability to the UK, but this book demonstrates that such a move would be hasty and to the detriment of children's well-being. As the results come in, the constant question remains: what happens to children when their parents are harshly sanctioned? To review the

FIGURE 1.1: **Characteristics of US Public Law 104.193 Personal Responsibility and Work Opportunity Reconciliation Act, also known as 'Welfare Reform'**

Main provisions of the legislation

- Temporary Assistance to Needy Families (TANF)
- Devolution of responsibility from central government to individual states with funding mechanism through Federal block grants, capped at each state's level of need in 1994.
- Federal funding of day care dependent on state legislation and implementation.
- Adults in families personally responsible to find work in all circumstances.
- Focus is on work as the solution to poverty.
- Disincentives to work removed (transitional funds for day care and health coverage to be provided).

- Work is preferable to time devoted to education.
- 60 months time limit on benefits for life, no entitlement.
- Sanctions (reduction in benefits as penalty for non-compliance) are key form of enforcement.
- Job counsellors have some discretion over what is considered legitimate work-related activity.
- Welfare reform applies to the system and local agency change.

- Emphasis is on lone women with children, who are referred to as 'jobseekers.'
- Unmarried teenagers are required to live with parents if seeking assistance.
- Benefits to immigrants are restricted.
- Incentives are provided to states to meet job placement goals.
- Some funding of research on effects of reforms.
- Narrowing of eligibility for supplemental security income for children with disabilities.

See Appendix 4 for excerpts from the legislation.

policy and to question the 'reforms' does not deny that they have been effective in some ways and this book asks what is transferable and what should be treated with extreme caution.

It is generally recognized that the UK and the US have maintained a special relationship historically, through the process of colonial independence, alliance through World Wars and NATO, shared language and common legislative and administrative practices. Thus, despite the fact that their contemporary economies and demographics are quite different, the apparent claims of success in the US Welfare Reform have attracted much attention from British policymakers, and the following pages analyze the basis for this attention.

Close ties between the US and UK do not mean complete uniformity between them. Indeed, as will be discussed in Chapters 2 and 4, the two allies vary considerably in their history of attitudes toward people experiencing poverty and in their approaches to central government involvement in social policy . For example, in 1991, 26 per cent of children in the US were reported to be in poverty before assistance and 22 per cent remained so after receiving government assistance.[3] For the UK, 30 per cent of children were in poverty before assistance and 10 per cent remained in poverty after government assistance. In a report funded by the same foundation in 1999, statistics from state to state give 'profiles of child well-being' and illuminate the consequences for children in families without adequate housing, nutrition, health coverage, adult support : '13 per cent, or 9.2 million, of our children are growing up with a collection of disadvantages that could curtail, if not scuttle, their chances to become productive adult participants in the mainstream of America's future.'[4]

Now, for the first time since the 1935 'New Deal' Aid to Dependent Children legislation in the US, American families will be turned away if they have used up five years' worth of benefits. For some teenage mothers, this means that by their early to mid 20s, their time is up for life since they will no longer be eligible for economic assistance; they can no longer depend on government exercising responsibility for their, or their children's, welfare should they not be able to work for a living. The five-year clock started ticking in many US states in 1997, so that by the year 2002 – or sooner for Pennsylvania – there will be some harsh consequences. The State of Oregon is the only legislature to have negotiated (at the time of writing in 2000) open-ended benefits rather than the five-year cut-off.

As will be discussed in Chapter 3, the importance of people's participation in the workforce for self-esteem and family efficacy has long been recognized and encouraged, particularly for women. However, the lack of choices and safety net for the poorest families with young children (under five) puts many at risk. Middle class women have long had, and continue to have, the choice to combine periods of infant care with reliance on their husbands' income or part-time work; parents of very young children experiencing poverty (predominantly women heads of households in both the US and the UK) have not had that choice. The US Welfare Reform perpetuates this lack of attention to the complexities of combining child-raising, low paid work and lack of educational opportunity with lone parenting.

Since the Second World War, and the major social policy legislation of 1945–48, the UK has been more thoroughly committed to integrated services for families, including health care and income maintenance, than the US. Despite the variation in interpretation of the concept 'Welfare State', two historical trends are shared:

(a) the tension between assigning poverty to structural reasons versus blaming the individual for their lack of wealth; and

(b) the failure of universal policies such as the 'New Deal' in the US and the 'Welfare State' in the UK to provide a safety net that maintains income (although it can be argued that the health and education components of the Welfare State in the UK have been successful in maintaining the health and literacy of children).

Some US policymakers and many in the media blame poverty on individual incapacity and wilful refusal to participate 'responsibly' in a complex society. It seems that the UK is being drawn back into an approach that it embraced with the Poor Law Reforms of the 1830s and moved away from in the aftermath of the First World War and more comprehensively at the end of the Second World War. As outlined in David Bull's Foreword, the term 'welfare' has been used to mean different things either side of the ocean. For the UK, especially since the Second World War, the Welfare State has referred to a group of social policies intended to maintain the basic well-being of citizens, especially in relation to education, health, personal social services, housing and income. Certainly the cost and intent of these programmes were attacked during the Thatcher years, but the words hold broad connotations of well-being, including the local vernacular of 'being on the welfare'. For the US 'welfare' is a much narrower concept of 'public assistance' for individuals who are unemployed, usually conflated with lone parents in the media image of 'welfare moms'. Chapter 2 discusses the narrower US version, but it is a constant strain throughout the debate on welfare reform, since too much has been taken for granted by the implication of shared meaning.

We restate David Bull's reminder that for the UK, the Welfare State was a collection of universally available, insurance or tax based benefits plus some means-tested or 'residual' benefits, generally administered centrally by a 'unitary' administration. For the US on the other hand, welfare reform refers to one slice of America's 'Reluctant Welfare State' and almost exclusively to that narrow band of means-tested income benefits, known since 1935 as Aid to Dependent Children (ADC), changed in 1950 to Aid to Families with Dependent Children (AFDC), which involved both federal and matched state funding (see timeline for policies of the US and UK, p39). Since 1996, welfare reform has meant new 'family investment programme' titles which are administered by individual states with bureaucratic arrangements increasingly devolved from central to local government and wide variation of benefits from state to state. These distinctions in the use of language which frames welfare as collective well-being or individual dependence are reflected in the different policy histories of the UK and US and the way people in receipt of public assistance are viewed.

A clear understanding of the different use of language in the US and UK is critical to any discussion of welfare reform. Another is whether a shift can be made from the historic US emphasis, which still endures in the UK, on defining people without money as 'the poor' and somehow inferior, to recognition of the structural elements that make the experience of poverty a crisis in contemporary survival for families and children. Certainly research in the US has revealed structural components of poverty, from the Pittsburg Survey in 1904 through the revelations of Michael Harrington's *Poverty in America*[5] in the 1960s and the current work of poverty institutes, the Children's Defence Fund and scholars such as J J Wilson,[6] However, this research has been ignored throughout the 1970s and 1980s by the increasingly conservative voices of the Republican party and is barely remembered even now with a Democratic President in power.

The UK has a more established awareness that poverty is structural – indeed, Chapter 4 argues that an unquestioned commitment to re-structuring society for the welfare of all existed following the Second World War – as demonstrated in the research of groups such as the CPAG and the Dartington Social Research Unit. However, the neo-conservatism of the Thatcher and Major years has left a stubborn resistance to the structural perspective and a readiness to blame the individual exclusively. Nevertheless, it is only when this shift is made, to seeing the structural issues that contribute to inadequate income, either in media stories or formal analysis of research, that it becomes possible for all of us to identify with the challenges of child poverty. People experiencing poverty become people from our street, in our neighbourhood, on our estate, in our village – 'us,' not 'them'.

In the current complex marketplace of layoffs, down turns and global economic ripple effects, very few individuals can risk assuming that they are invulnerable to crises in income maintenance at some point in their lives. Beyond this recognition that all of us are potentially vulnerable, there must also be acknowledgement of the contributions made everyday by people who are poor to the well-being of all (for example by part-time employees or those in below-minimum-wage occupations such as the service industries, domestic help, janitorial). Traditional approaches to helping people experiencing poverty have been relentlessly demeaning and have undervalued the abilities of people going through hard times. Yet, people who have endured poverty manifest resilience, ingenuity and the ability to raise children, despite the faulty systems surrounding them.[7] To discount people in poverty as a social drain is to stigmatize and exclude citizens, most of whom are children, from the collective endeavour of building healthy and creative communities for future generations. As a young German Jew, Albert Einstein narrowly missed the holocaust. Children in poverty face their own foreclosed[8] future at who knows what loss of potential to society. There are more African American males between 18 and 22 in US prisons than in colleges and the majority are from poor neighbourhoods. Is the UK record any better? Michael Little's book *Young Men in Prison*, gives insight into the development of an educationally deprived, criminal and anti-social identity.[9]

The loss of potential of those children whose future is foreclosed by poverty is one matter for policy makers to consider, another is the ever-ready stereotyping of people experiencing poverty as lazy adults. While there are certainly examples of able-bodied adults, without dependents, who choose not to seek work, they are not typical of people experiencing poverty in either the US or the UK. The overwhelming majority of welfare recipients are the children of lone parents (see p49, figure 3.1). A scrutiny of social provisions demonstrates that narrow policies have in the past trapped people in poverty, and low wages have produced a disincentive for some families to enter the formal workplace. Moreover, the history, value-judgements and realities of poverty are many layered, and must be considered.

A central goal for this book is to establish the complexity and relevance for UK legislators of the 1996–97 'US Welfare Reform' policies and the current implementation process. During a review of policy history, design, implementation, political pressures, consequences particularly for children, and current legislation concerning poverty in the US, questions will be raised including:

- How does the US Welfare Reform stand as an anti-poverty strategy?
- What are the implications for children in poor families?
- Which parts of the reform are most effective?
- Is the emphasis on employment at all costs feasible?
- Which elements are damaging?
- Is this move from welfare to work more for political effect than raising people out of poverty?

These questions helped to frame the objectives of the book as follows:

OBJECTIVES

1. To identify the issues concerning children in poverty and their families.
2. To reach a critical understanding of US and UK approaches to poverty and income maintenance, highlighting what may work and what is likely to be an unproductive transplanting of ideas.
3. To recognize the goals of US style 'welfare reform', distinguishing between elements which are politically driven (that is, vote-catching and meant to support the status and control of wealth of the middle and upper class) and those which are anti-poverty strategies.
4. To provide documented evidence of policy makers' 'success' in reaching their goals especially where they relate to children.
5. To give an insight into the unintended consequences of welfare reform on children.
6. To formulate recommendations for action by British policy makers'.

While Chapters 2 to 5 focus specifically on US social welfare history, current US welfare reform, UK welfare history and reform, transferability and recommendations, these six objectives above will be introduced briefly here and are woven throughout the book.

OBJECTIVE I – TO IDENTIFY THE ISSUES CONCERNING CHILDREN IN POVERTY AND THEIR FAMILIES

To achieve an understanding of the challenges confronting policymakers trying to reduce child poverty, progress reports from individual states, social science research and current US national statistics will be reviewed. For example, the Washington Center on

Budget and Policy Priorities 1997 report[10] confirms that, despite strong economic growth,

> The income disparity between the top fifth of families with children and families at the bottom of the income scale has grown substantially over the last two decades...on average, incomes of the *richest fifth of families increased* by 30 per cent, or nearly $27,000. In sharp contrast, *incomes of the poorest fifth of families and children decreased* in 44 states in this period...the decline in real incomes of the poorest families with children averaged $2,500.00.

Furthermore, tax policies for the richest ten per cent of Americans have been relaxing in the same years that penalties for those in poverty, particularly children, have been tightening. The accumulated tax breaks in the Reagan years since 1980 meant that, by 1997,

> The top 10 per cent of the population (in the US) owned 73.2 per cent of the nation's net worth, up from 68 per cent in 1983...Looked at from the other side of the Income Gap, we find that those in the bottom 20 per cent have actually lost ground in the '90s.[11]

Thus, in a time of unprecedented growth, some elusive factors worked against society being able to 'lift all boats' with the rising tide at the close of the last century. At a time when it would be most expected that child poverty could be reduced, it is as thorny a problem as ever. One contradiction is that while the contemporary workforce is increasingly *technology driven, competitive and well educated*, the emphasis in US income maintenance policy is on the individual's responsibility to find a job, any job, sometimes without adequate educational support. Workforce participation of adults is an important element in tackling child poverty, but it cannot stand alone.

The transition from workless to workpoor is the reality where people enter lowest paid and minimal qualification positions in both the US and the UK.[12] There are short-term arguments that more education does not necessarily mean improved access to work; however, the evidence is conflicting as demonstrated in the success of the Phillips 'Project for Pride in Living' in Minnesota and the State of Maryland workforce participation report.[13] What is clear, is that in the long term, only people who have had opportunity for re-training and education will be able to command positions that raise them above the minimum wage in the 'technically sophisticated workforce' discussed in the US WorkForce 2020 Report.[14]

In addition to training and education, those recipients of income maintenance who are parents of young children (*the majority* of recipients of the former Aid to Families with Dependent Children: AFDC and current welfare-to-work programmes) also need stable and affordable housing, access to transport, child care, healthcare and social supports.[15] As will be discussed in Chapter 3, welfare recipients are not the block of able-bodied idle people portrayed in the media. One approach does not meet all needs. Policy makers have emphasized the dependency created by former welfare provision and have claimed that requiring work outside the home mitigates the danger of becoming dependent on the state. While returning to work outside the home may provide work place values for older children and teenagers, it means nothing to children under the age of three. For babies and toddlers, or in Jackson and Goldschmied's words 'people under three', periods of social opportunity may aid children's development, but their primary need is for a parent who is wholly focused on the child's well-being, survival through childhood ailments, social and emotional hurdles to entering school, and healthy physical development, rather than on the demands of full-time employment.[16] Many families currently receiving income maintenance in the US and the UK have more than one child under five years. A crucial concern for any new welfare legislation, then, is to *recognize the differing groups of people involved and their differing opportunities and needs.* To limit special distinctions in implementation to able-bodied adults, the mentally ill or disabled is not enough, especially when the future well-being of children is at stake.

Lone parenting with young children is hard work in itself. Both the US National Commission on Children and the UK National Children's Bureau stress the importance of stable care-giving in the home, particularly during the first years of life. The reality on both sides of the Atlantic shows a failure to achieve this. Within the UK,

- Lone parents comprise the greatest proportion of families living in poverty – over half (63 per cent) live in poverty.
- Couples with children account for the largest number of people in poverty (4.7 million).
- The average number of families falling into poverty across all family types is 23 per cent.

Furthermore, income inequality is increasing:

- Average income has increased by 44 per cent.
- Since 1979 the poorest 10 per cent have seen a fall of 9 per cent in their real income.
- The richest 10 per cent have seen a rise of 70 per cent in their income.
- Women and children are more likely than men to have persistent low incomes.[17]

Encouraging the take-up of any job simply to 'get off the rolls' does not address the needs of children. If middle and upper class homemakers have always been excused from the workforce when child-raising, why is it so hard to extend this value to the poor?[18] What is it in the history of welfare policy that has created conditions of blame and punitive approaches for those who fail to accumulate wealth? Parents, and therefore children, are being 'sanctioned' (deprived of benefits) for not finding work quickly enough. This at a time when the market for low skilled people is shrinking and the capacity of people to survive 'independently' in a complex workplace is limited without co-ordinated levels of support from employers, trainers, counsellors and funding for education. The best hope of US welfare legislation is the involvement of corporations in employee training to bridge the gaps, plus an increased investment by government in housing, transportation, child care, education and health coverage. Another hope regarding welfare reform is that the debate renews public awareness of the issues and how the well-being of everyone suffers as long as children in need are neglected. The city of Philadelphia, for example, is currently experiencing a *'welfare crisis'*; the repercussions of sanctions on children are dire:

> Those children are scarred. They weren't born that way. But we're failing them. One of those kids is the next Einstein, you know? And we're losing them all. Every one of them.[19]

The consequences of welfare reform are still being evaluated, but questions from interim reports include: what are the realities for parents and for their children when they meet the newly enacted time limits and deadlines for cut off in 2002 (and even earlier in some states such as Pennsylvania)? How can transport to work be made easier? What is happening to recent immigrants? Where does the language of 'sanctions' for people who fail to meet the work requirements come from and why is it so punishing? All these questions are crucial in the analysis of how appropriate, transferable, or welcome any part of the welfare reform is in the UK. While the US has one of the most productive economies in the world, the gap between rich and poor is the widest on the planet: 'Since 1985 the richest five per cent of American families have received a larger share of the nation's income than the poorest 40 per cent.'[20] The figures suggest that the UK is already on a similar path, but effective child poverty legislation could challenge such growing disparities.

OBJECTIVE 2 – TO REACH A CRITICAL UNDERSTANDING OF US AND UK APPROACHES TO POVERTY AND INCOME MAINTENANCE, HIGHLIGHTING WHAT MAY WORK AND WHAT IS LIKELY TO BE AN UNPRODUCTIVE TRANSPLANTING OF IDEAS

The uneven history of approaches to tackling poverty is discussed further in Chapter 2 for the US and in Chapter 4 for the UK. However, a key difference between the UK and the US is the constant undercurrent of resistance to 'big government' in the US as intrusive in people's lives. The Republican party continues to base its principles on the reduction of government and policy interference in the creation of wealth. The Democratic party is more disposed to the traditional Founding Fathers' definition of government: 'We the people by the people'. It must, nevertheless, always tread the fine line between maintaining government responsibility for collective well-being while still appealing to the notion of individual control. Certainly the myth of the freedom of the individual to sink or swim and the individualism of the 'American Dream' (that anyone can be free to make their fortune, to be a pioneer) has had a major impact on the collective commitment to tackling child poverty. In the UK, collective approaches to resolving poverty have been widely accepted since the end of the First World War when successful campaigns promoted policies establishing public housing – such as the 'Homes fit for heroes' campaign – and ensuring children received an adequate diet.

   Although in the UK many influences came to bear on attitudes towards poverty down the centuries, it was not until the early twentieth century that the blaming of individuals was seriously questioned. Throughout the nineteenth century there had been a series of reactions to poor law reforms which paved the way to more sympathetic attitudes to need, for example in the shaming books of Dickens and in the railings of Disraeli against the harsh reforms of the

1830s. The discussions of the Trade Union Congress of 1888 had also raised the plight of those on low wages, and the Seebohm Rowntree book, *Poverty: A Study of Town Life*, had captured Winston Churchill's attention to such an extent that he wrote to his colleagues in 1902:

> I have been reading a book which has fairly made my hair stand on end, dealing with poverty in the town of York…and which I strongly recommend you to read. It is quite evident from the figures which he adduces that the American labourer is a stronger, larger, healthier, better fed, and consequently more efficient animal than a large proportion of our population, and this is surely a fact which our unbridled Imperialists, who have no thought but to pile up armaments, taxation and territory, should not lose sight of. For my own part, I see little glory in an Empire which can rule the waves, and is unable to flush its own sewers. [21]

However, it was the 1909 War Budget which most clearly articulated the structural aspects of poverty. In his budget speech to Parliament, Lloyd George gained the derision of the opposition party who were hoping to increase the defence and military budget, but enlightened many to the fact that poverty was not to be blamed entirely on the individual:

> What are the dominating causes of poverty amongst the industrial classes?…old age, premature breakdown in health and strength, the death of the breadwinner, and unemployment due either to the decay of industries and seasonable demands, or to the fluctuations or depressions in trade…This is a War Budget. It is for raising money to wage implacable warfare against poverty and squalidness. I cannot help hoping and believing that before this generation has passed away we shall have advanced a great step towards that good time when poverty, and wretchedness and human degradation which always follow in its camp…' [22]

For the US during this past century, there was a brief period of recognition of wider societal and 'structural' reasons of poverty, beyond the control of the individual, that called for a massive mobilization of public resources akin to a war. Most writers refer to President L B Johnson's *War on Poverty* of the 1960s, and the successful anti-poverty programme 'Head Start' among others, as the example of a time when Americans began to come to grips with the realities of poverty as a collective concern. Gains in tackling poverty and ill-health included significant reductions in the infant mortality rate (33 per cent reduction between 1965 and 1975) which were ignored by later critics of this period.[23] Researchers and politicians of that decade documented the vulnerability of people when there are shifts in the employment sector or institutions that perpetuate racism or sexism in hiring policies.[24] However, the gains in political attention and social acceptance for government intervention on behalf of people's welfare were eclipsed in the late 1960s by the crisis of the Vietnam War and became buried with the conservative voices linking economic success with tax reduction in the 1980s and 1990s. Welfare policies became punitive as a concerted backlash against welfare rights organizations, for the first time requiring that mothers of young children work rather than care for their children at home.

Recognition that the roots of poverty are structural has not taken hold for long in the US, where the dominating theme continues in the first decade of 2000 to be economic independence and opportunity for the individual: opportunity to be both rich and poor. It is very clear what the message is concerning the current 'welfare reform' legislation: as stated in the Minnesota State guidelines, this policy is a 'tough but fair solution to dependency'.[25] The Minnesota Family Investment Program (MFIP – the state's version of welfare reform) notes 'the intent of MFIP is to help you find work as soon as possible. Most families can only stay on MFIP for 60 months. So it is important that you act quickly to become self-sufficient.' In the media, the emphasis is on promoting individual responsibility and curtailing the negative behaviours of the assumed majority of people in poverty. While no one could disagree with the notion of personal responsibility to make the best of opportunities, to recipients these slogans have often increased feelings of judgement and stigma as detailed in the case studies in Chapter 3 and the words of people experiencing poverty.[26]

Historical trends blaming individuals for their plight rather than acknowledging structural reasons for poverty are powerful and will be explored in the context of exclusion and inclusion in Chapter 2. It is important to note how deep seated these attitudes are. At a recent conference in Minnesota, Professor Mary Ann Brenden introduced her paper on US welfare reform by identifying the characteristics of the policy as follows:

- each family should take care of its own
- work is the solution
- localities are responsible

- residency requirements for eligibilty
- lesser eligibility[27]

Participants discussed how they experienced each of these characteristics in the current legislation and then to the ironic laughter of the group, Professor Brenden reminded the audience that these are the principles of the 1601 Elizabethan Poor Laws. The researcher Joel Handler goes further and cites the 1349 Statute of Laborers as the first time these responses to poverty were introduced: 'Welfare policy still lies in the shadow of the sturdy beggar' where poor single mothers are considered unworthy.[28] The historic emphasis on lazy people, refusing to work continues, but Handler notes, 'to frame welfare reform policy in terms of moving recipients from welfare to the paid labor force is to fail to define the problem'. This framing continues to punish the victims of poverty, especially children. When the blame is laid on those in poverty, questions do not have to be addressed concerning who those in poverty are, why and what their needs are. Handler sounds out utterly clear warnings: 'If welfare officials get too tough on mothers, state and local governments will have to pick up the pieces – more impoverishment, more need for health care, more broken homes, more children in foster care…'[29]

OBJECTIVE 3 – TO RECOGNIZE THE GOALS OF US STYLE 'WELFARE REFORM', DISTINGUISHING BETWEEN ELEMENTS WHICH ARE POLITICALLY DRIVEN (THAT IS, VOTE-CATCHING AND MEANT TO SUPPORT THE STATUS AND CONTROL OF WEALTH OF THE MIDDLE AND UPPER CLASS) AND THOSE WHICH ARE ANTI-POVERTY STRATEGIES

The centrepiece of US welfare reform legislation is the moving of people from 'welfare dependency' to work. This makes sense to many and there are clearly work programs which are successful, as documented by the McKnight Foundation and the Manpower Development Research Corporation.[30] Set alongside successes are the barriers to getting 'off welfare':

- low wages compared to the cost of living (26 per cent respondents);
- limited education and limited opportunity to get more (20 per cent respondents); and
- lack of child care that is flexible, affordable, reliable (18 per cent).

(respondents comprised 395 current and former recipients and 69 employers).[31]

In a recent study of 948 women in California, Connecticut and Florida, entitled *Remember the Children*, an additional concern is that affordable childcare is often (33 per cent of respondents) offered by untrained friends, neighbours, kin. While some family arrangements work well, the researchers document that:

> These home-based providers fell below the average quality level of center-based programs. We observed fewer educational materials, much greater use of television and videos, and unclean facilities. In short, we find that the welfare-to-work push on single mothers is placing a growing number of children in mediocre and disorganized child care settings.[32]

Thus, the concern remains that success rates are exaggerated, particularly when considering the complex consequences for women trying to re-enter the workplace with two or three children under five. In the complex job market of the 1990s and technology driven workplace, education and flexible employment skills are the keys to success; but education has been omitted or deliberately ignored in the current legislation because of costs.

Although the outlook for the current US welfare legislation is bleak for the poorest and youngest children, there are elements which have raised public attention and which may eventually lead to the shift in public opinion from blame to concerted action for those who, for a variety of reasons, are not participating in work outside the home. For legislation concerning 'welfare reform' or a true 'New Deal' to be more than another round of blaming the victim and to become a true anti-poverty strategy, structural issues need to be addressed, including the following:

- Access to higher education and training
- Prevention of teenage pregnancy
- Provision of child care
- review of the camouflaged occupational welfare of able-bodied middle class women choosing to be homemakers
- Recognition of homemaking and care of your own children under five as 'work'
- Housing
- Health coverage
- Transport

The last three items have received more government attention and funding in the UK than in the US since 1947. Of the first five only child care has received detailed attention and funding and only in some States. Access to higher education for people on low incomes has been neglected. Meanwhile, the resources enjoyed by able-bodied middle class homemakers have been ignored; they continue to receive 'fiscal welfare' in terms of tax deductions for their husbands and their mortgages, without social stigma.[33] In the light of this omission and the current media frenzy of labelling those in poverty as dependent, unworthy and a drain, it is important to review our personal and professional attitudes towards poverty. Handler suggests that 'welfare policy is not addressed to the poor – it is addressed to us. It is an affirmation of majoritarian values through the creation of deviants...the poor are held hostage to make sure the rest of us behave...'[34] Certainly within the US the current language of dependency and 'sanctions' is harsh enough to give everyone pause to avoid going back to the Elizabethan Poor Laws. However, for children there is no choice.

OBJECTIVE 4 – TO PROVIDE DOCUMENTED EVIDENCE OF POLICY MAKERS' 'SUCCESS' IN REACHING THEIR GOALS ESPECIALLY WHERE THEY RELATE TO CHILDREN

Despite these harsh realities and the punitive nature of 'sanctions', there are innovations in US welfare reform legislation that can be usefully transplanted and as many as possible of them will be identified in this book. For example, welfare reform has created new connections between social services and the private sector. Social workers in the US are helping to connect clients to work training and employment opportunities as conditions for maintaining income support. There are innovations including corporate involvement and opportunities for training collaboratives of the kind laid out in the McKnight Foundation papers, *22 Partnerships Get Down to Business*. There is also increased attention and public-private funding for co-operative child care facilities, and health care provision.

This is a crucial time to ask UK politicians and public to review critically the so-called 'successes' of US style welfare reform. While the dialogue has sparked important attention and a re-framing of the debates toward the question of employment and public-private partnerships, the methods of moving people from welfare to work are

Dickensian: get it together (with the supports provided by voluntary as well as public agencies) or get out of our (state income maintenance offices) sight if your life is not in order within the set time limits. Voluntary agencies, such as the Salvation Army, charities and church organizations have set up supports for parents in transition from work in the home to full-time employment, but there is already a tension building; they cannot fill the gaps and will not be able to cope when families with children have their income cut. For parents who began parenting in their teens, sanctions are being imposed before their mid-20s. Mayor Rendell describes the impact of arbitrary time limits for the City of Philadelphia, as catastrophic:

> A growing number of voices are saying that Philadelphia is not due for a welfare reform crisis. Let me dissuade you of this myth. Literally thousands of mothers and children are likely to become penniless after the state's two-year time limit on welfare benefits kicks in...[35]

The State of Oregon has already recognized that those who are not succeeding in the workforce or have too many home responsibilities to survive full-time employment, will be accumulating in welfare caseloads in the next few years and have therefore negotiated more flexible deadlines and extensions.

The irony in this current saga of US welfare reform which has been unfolding since the 1996 Personal Responsibility and Work Opportunity Reconciliation Act was passed by Congress and implemented in 1997, is that there are reports of huge success, for example in 'getting people back to work' or 'off the rolls' at the same time that there is an impending sense of disaster for those who will be destitute. There are some clear examples of the positive results of this legislation, of lives that have taken on renewed meaning when people have re-entered the workplace with proper support and improved income as detailed in Chapter 3. The crisis lies in the reality that it is children who are 'cut-off' from supports when their parents are cut off and that too often 'off the rolls' does not mean earning a living wage. It may mean earning a better wage but at terrible cost in terms of less-than-ideal child care for children under five and less time to parent.

Although it makes sense for the Blair government to look at the experience of other countries and particularly across the Atlantic, there are multiple issues for analysis, including both dangers and opportunities. These are summarized in figure 1.3 (p24). Among the dangers, chiefly, is the desire to find ready-made, politically attractive and speedy answers at the risk of missing the opportunity to improve the longer term economic standards for children living in poverty. Moreover, the strategy preferred in the US of cutting costs by reducing benefits and imposing sanctions will boomerang in the future costs to society of families being put under pressure and torn apart. Certainly there are many negative repercussions for young children in the current US policy, but there are also innovations which can be used by legislators in the UK, especially in terms of linking up with a variety of resources both private and public in the community and expanding corporate involvement.

OBJECTIVE 5 – TO GIVE AN INSIGHT INTO THE UNINTENDED CONSEQUENCES OF WELFARE REFORM ON CHILDREN

The persistence of poverty despite extreme wealth in the US is both puzzling and sickening, especially where it means that children are destitute from the moment they begin life. Perhaps there is a higher 'threshold' of tolerating poverty in the US than in the UK because of the widespread dream that anyone can achieve millionaire, if not billionaire, status and that the greatest freedom an individual has is the right to fail or succeed. US welfare reform has elements that seem to tackle well-being in constructive ways, for example: encouraging public-private partnerships in offering social supports to families; promoting corporate responsibility and involvement in job training and preparation; heightening awareness of the experience of poverty, etc. Yet, it also has the unintended consequence of compounding the criminalization of the poor for their economic and social conditions, their failure to secure employment and their further failure to comply to tight stipulations and deadlines. When parents, especially those with children under five years of age, are unable to sustain employment or are not supported by employers in their family responsibilities, their children are the first to suffer.

The major concern, then, is that sanctioning adults for their failure to find work (for example, in Minnesota by cutting benefits by 10 per cent and then 30 per cent) has a direct impact on children's well-being. Furthermore, it ignores the United Nations Convention on the Rights of the Child – that every child have food, shelter, safety and opportunity to grow and develop in a healthy way.[36] A visiting Professor from Eastern Europe commented, in a lecture to US graduate students concerning child poverty, 'such destitution would not be experienced in Slovenia; we used to have full employment and even as we change from a socialist to a mixed economy, we live with the expectation that we provide for one another'.[37] Shelters for the homeless that are now brimming with children, or the soup kitchens that exist across the US, illustrate the sense of uselessness, loss of identity and autonomy those excluded from the national aura of well-being are made to feel.

It would appear, therefore, that US policy defines welfare reform as another way of attacking the poor, and most especially lone parents, mainly women, already struggling to survive motherhood in a era where corporate executives earn at ever increasing levels.[38] Even if we may question the United Nations' commitment to a child's right to grow and develop in safety, the practical repercussions of neglecting children's well-being reverberate on everyone. In the quad at Toynbee Hall in the East End of London, there is a statue of Jane Addams, the American social activist and founder of Hull House in Chicago. Jane Addams valued and built upon the exchange of ideas between the US and the UK; she also said 'the wealth of the individual is precarious and uncertain until it is founded on the well-being of us all and incorporated into our common life'.[39]

Reform in the US is being re-framed as renewal when for some it will mean increased exclusion. The elements of US welfare reform that appeal to UK policy makers, such as the 'Wisconsin success' and the consequences for children of such reform, need to be examined, made known and avoided. These include the 'astonishing disparities of family income state-by-state, 20-1 in New York, almost 30-1 in the District of Columbia...on a scale from lowest to highest income' (Center on Budget Priorities); over-flowing homeless shelters for women and children in Minnesota; and extremes of child poverty in the Mississippi Delta.[40] Recently, in an article entitled 'Some children bear brunt of changes in welfare system', Hopfensperger identified the paradox that for some the welfare reforms have worked well, while for the frailest families they have caused a downward spiral in survival:

> When Minnesota's welfare overhaul was launched more than a year ago, proponents predicted that children would benefit from seeing their mothers work and enjoying a bigger family income.
>
> For many families, that has happened. But the welfare overhaul also has prompted an explosion in the use of crisis nurseries, tremendous stress on fragile families, and a pool of about 3,500 families each month whose

welfare benefits have been reduced – and whose children are left in vulnerable conditions…the new welfare system inadvertently has left some parents with terrible choices.[41]

A key distinction has to be made between reforming a bureaucratic system that may be wasteful and may have had doubtful impact in the past, with claiming that a revised policy such as the current US welfare reform is an anti-poverty strategy. In the US it is clear that the welfare system, with its centre piece of Aid to Dependent Children, later Aid to Families with Dependent Children, needed revision. However, for political, historical, social and economic reasons, the current reform seems to fall far short of attacking poverty. The removal of a 'safety net' and the imposition of sanctions in the form of benefit cuts may be directed at the adults who fail to get or sustain work, but the net effect, for children in particular, is 'less cereal and heat at the end of the month' and an under-resourced, fragile community life.[42]

There is a book in the US entitled *There are no children here* by Alex Kotlowitz, which depicts life for two young brothers through several summers in the Chicago 'projects'.[43] On reading it, one needs to keep checking the dates, 1991, 1992, to be convinced that this is not part of ancient history. These creative, capable, loyal boys spend their days avoiding gun fire and losing their grip on a sense of future, they discuss the colour of silks in coffins and not *when* they grow up but *if*. In an era of such plenty, it should be possible to ensure that children can grow and develop in peace. The poverty of children in Chicago has not been a direct result of current welfare reform legislation; however, the focus of the new legislation on parents going back to work or facing sanctions in work-starved communities means that many children are worse off.[44] In Britain, there are towns in the Midlands, Wales and the South West devastated by economic dislocation and plant closings. Communities such as Hartcliffe in Bristol have few opportunities for school leavers, prevalent teenage pregnancy, and high levels of poverty amongst children. The challenges of surviving in such an environment are vividly depicted in the works of Owen Gill and Christine Stones.[45]

OBJECTIVE 6 – TO FORMULATE RECOMMENDATIONS FOR BRITISH POLICY MAKERS' ACTION

For the UK, beginning a new millennium with a new administration in place and a growing economy, there is a window of opportunity to be powerfully effective in attacking poverty. However, the balance and focus are tightly contained in a political agenda. No one argues with the idea that we must do better when confronted with the hunger of children in an era of spectacular technological and scientific growth. However, in an environment which honours corporate enterprise and the marketplace above human well-being, costs are defined differently: costs to taxpayers are interpreted by some as harming the middle and upper classes ability to invest; costs to children left in hunger mean community loss of potential at least, epidemics and violence at worst – ultimately these latter are costs to us all.

Colleagues at the University of the West Indies, Mona, Jamaica, addressed a colloquium of social policy analysts and social workers at Orlando, Florida, in 1998 and warned them that if the rich focus only on investing and acquiring wealth for themselves, social divisions are always the result. They criticized the Structural Adjustment Programs (SAPs) of the International Monetary Fund and asked their audience to note the parallels of US style 'welfare reform' with SAPs and their impact in restricting even further the resources that go into impoverished communities.[46] The message is clear: none of us is secure while some of us are hungry. None of us can truly experience well-being while some of us are excluded. There is a housing complex in Hackney, North London with high walls surrounding it – not a prison but a courtyard of wealthy residences that need protecting. Similarly across the US, the gated, secure communities of Boca Raton in Florida are spreading. Bricks and mortar do not bring social security; effective anti-poverty strategies could.

Frank Field, when Minister for Welfare Reform, cautioned against a 'quick fix'. His concerns that we cannot simply graft what seems to work in one place to another are well-founded[47]. As Field has warned everyone in Britain not to go in for the 'Big Bang' theory of welfare reform, this book also emphasizes that reasoned effective reform takes time and careful preparation despite the political pressures and realities of the negotiation table. There are many resistant, difficult issues which will be included in the debate, and this book will highlight several of them, with a particular emphasis on learning from the US 'welfare reform' experiment and providing suggestions and insights for effective anti-poverty strategies. US welfare policy has been a failure in key particulars within its own context and the UK government can benefit from paying attention to these failures.

Clearly there are no simple solutions to the problems children face when they are raised in poverty. A balance has to be found between policy that works, without appearing too costly to taxpayers, and policy that needs to be amended. An example in the US of hastily amended policy can be seen in the limitation and later reinstatement of food stamps for legal immigrants following the suicides of elderly Hmong people (refugees and immigrants to the US from northern Cambodia where they had helped military intelligence in the Vietnam war). This book offers both critical analysis and practical examples of elements of the US welfare reform which have been welcomed, have sparked innovation and positive energy and those elements which continue to fail children in poverty.

Internationally the USA is seen as a model of corporate and technological success. The economic climate is booming, executive salaries are so high that it is not remarkable that people like Al Chechi (former Northwest Airlines CEO) can spend $3 million of his personal finances on his unsuccessful campaign to become Governor of California. Unemployment in the US is low and the national debt is contained. However, the question asked in relation to welfare reform is how we assess the 'success' of a country, by its economy and wealthy 10 per cent or by the quality of life for its children? In 1997 the *Times* published an article entitled: 'Welfare Isn't Working – But Will Anything Else?'; It discussed the soaring costs of welfare in European countries and pointed out that the US is second only to Japan as the lowest spender of fourteen industrialized countries, not including Canada which has always outspent the US, particularly in healthcare support. It is a doubtful source of political pride to be the lowest spender when children remain in need.

Currently in the US there is an uneasy divide. Quality of life for corporate executives (usually white and male) is booming. Quality of life for welfare recipients with dependent children (usually women and increasingly Black women) is worsening. In her work *Families in Peril*, Marion Wright Edelman of the Children's Defense Fund reports that one in two Black children are in poverty.[48] Current reports are consistently saying that children are faring worse not better as a result of this legislation in the US. The challenge is therefore: how can the UK avoid the major criticisms of US welfare reform that are now widespread and yet simultaneously benefit from its advances in bringing people to the workplace and alerting private enterprise to its role in achieving social inclusion?

Despite the success statistics concerning reductions in 'welfare rolls', the emphasis in the US is on individual responsibility and entering the job market at a time when the market for low-skilled people is

FIGURE 1.3: **The characteristics, concerns and opportunities of the Personal Responsibility and Work Opportunity Reconciliation Act, also known as 'Welfare Reform'**

POLICY PROVISION	CONCERN	OPPORTUNITY
• Policy targets adult individual	• shifts in labour market opportunity	• encourages job seeking from unskilled to skilled while former recipients are unskilled
• Focus is on work as the solution	• poverty is about more than work, including childcare, affordable housing, transport, access to jobs, teen pregnancy	• emphasis on participation in social norms of work
• Work is preferable to time in education	• education is costly but crucial to advance on any career ladder	• short-term salary gain over public asistance
• Sanctions are key form of enforcement	• cutting benefits for non-compliance directly attacks children's health and well-being, also stigmatizing	• action under threat
• Job counsellors have discretion	• too much power of decision and pressure to succeed with getting people into employment may jeopardise education planning and push people into dead-end jobs for the sake of 'getting them off the roll'	• make a relationship (even if power is unequal)
• Welfare reform applies to the system and to devolution	• there is confusion between welfare policy in the US which addresses system failures and strategies which attack the roots of poverty	• give more power to local justice • revitalize tired offices
• Emphasis is on single women with children	• the feminization of poverty is increased with current approaches to 'welfare reform'	• lessens isolation of women even while the policy reduces choices

shrinking so that simply moving people into low-paid jobs is a mirage of success. Furthermore, the capacity of people to survive 'independently' in a complex marketplace is low without co-ordinated levels of support from employers, trainers, counsellors and the public. In analyzing the intent of US welfare reform, this book unpeels the layers of beliefs, myths, values surrounding the complex issue of poverty. It asks what will be the realities for parents and for their children as the policy is implemented and they meet the 'limits' in 2002 and beyond.

Essentially the goal of this book is to demonstrate ways the UK can learn from the US policy changes without emulating them on the basis of short-term 'success data.' One of the main benefits of the 'welfare reform' debate is the way it brings often unpopular issues to the fore, highlighting, for example, the lack of resources going to children. Such debate also quickens our fragile grasp of economic community and interdependence. It is hoped that this information will raise awareness of both the complexity of welfare reform and the simplicity of the goal of anti-poverty strategies: to reduce child poverty.

NOTES

1 UNICEF *State of the World's Children*, Washington: UN (poverty: defined by the UN in absolute terms of access to adequate nutrition, housing, access to safe drinking water, clothing, protection, health services.), 1998.

2 R Greenstein, *Children in poverty report from the Center on Budget Policy and Priorities*, 1999. URL (or *Star Tribune*, 23 December 1999, pA4.)

3 Annie E Casey Foundation, *Kids Count*, p17, AECF, 1998.

4 L Rainwater and T Smeeding, Annie E. Casey Foundation, *Kids Count Data Book*, AECF, 1999, p5.

5 M Harrington, *The Other America: Poverty in the United States*, Vintage, 1962.

6 J J Wilson (1999), *When Work Disappears*, Vintage, 1999.

7 A Kotlowitz, *There are no children here*, Doubleday, 1991; O Gill, *Parenting Under Pressure*, Barnado's, 1992.

8 Prothrow-Stith, *Deadly Consequences*, Harper Collins, 1991.

9 M Little, *Young Men in Prison*, Aldershot: Dartmouth UK, 1990.

10 Center on Budget & Policy Priorities – *Pulling Apart: State Income Inequalities*, December 1997. URL: http://www.cbpp.org/pa/rel/htm

11 M Ivins, *Looking for ways to make the income gap worse*, Star-Telegram, 6 December, 1999.

12 Children's Defense Fund, *After Welfare, Many Families Fare Worse*, CDF, 1998; T MacDermott and A Garnham, *Real Choices for Lone Parents & their children*, CPAG, 1998.

13 State of Maryland, *Workforce Participation Report*, 1998.

14 Citizen's League, Workforce 2020 Report, Citizen's League, 1999.
15 Children's Defense, *Fund Welfare to What?* CDF, 1999.
16 S Jackson & E Goldschmied, *People Under Three*, 1998.
17 CPAG, Households Below Average Income in Facts & Figures, *Poverty*, Winter, No 105, CPAG, 2000, p21.
18 G Minks, *The Wages of Motherhood*, 1998.
19 D Cooper, *The Philadelphia Inquirer Magazine*, March, 1999.
20 Children's Defense Fund *State of America's Children CDF Yearbook*, CDF, 1998.
21 Churchill, (note 21).
22 R S Churchill, *Young Statesman, 1901–14 Winston S. Churchill*, Vol. II pp30–2, 1967, quoted in M Bruce, *The Rise of the Welfare State*, Weidenfeld and Nicolson, 1973.
23 T Wicker, *No Bread? Let 'em eat cake*, New York Times, September 1990.
24 J Handler, *The Poverty of Welfare Reform*, Yale University Press, 1995, p5.
25 Department of Human Service, *Guidelines to Welfare Reform*, St Paul, DHS, 1997.
26 P Beresford, D Green, R Lister and K Woodard, *Poverty First Hand: Poor People Speak for themselves*, CPAG, 1999.
27 M Brendan, *Update on Welfare Reform for Practitioners*. Presentation to the National Association of Social Workers. June 1998.
28 Handler, (note 25), p5.
29 Handler, (note 25), p8.
30 McKnight Foundation, *22 Partnerships Get Down to Business*, MKF, 1998.
31 McKnight Foundation, *How Welfare-to-work is working*, MKF, 2000, p8.
32 B Fuller & S Kagan, *Remember the children: Mothers Balance Work and Child Care Under Welfare Reform*, University of California, Berkeley and Yale University, Graduate School of Education–PACE University of California, Wave 1 Findings, 2000, p5.
33 R Titmuss, *Commitment to Welfare*, Pantheon, 1968.
34 Handler, (note 24), pp8–9.
35 E Rendell, *The Philadelphia Inquirer*, 3 March, 1999.
36 United Nations, *Convention on the Rights of the Child*, UNICEF, 1990.
37 G Cacinovic Vogrincic, Swapping courses with Slovenia, *Augsburg Now*, 1998.
38 M Abramovitz, *Regulating the Lives of Women*, 1995.
39 Jane Addams Papers, Swarthmore Peace Collection, *The Times*, 27 December, 1934.
40 Center on Budget & Policy Priorities – *Pulling Apart: State Income Inequalities*, December 1997. URL: http://www.cbpp.org/pa/rel/htm.
41 J Hopfensperger, *Star Tribune*, 27 February 1999.
42 Tammi, welfare recipient testimony, NASW, May 1998.
43 Kotlowitz, (note 7).
44 J J Wilson, *When Work Disappears*, Vintage, 1999.

45 C Stones, *Focus on Families: Family Centres in Action*, MacMillan Barnardos, 1994.

46 J Maxwell, *Poverty in the Caribbean*, Presentation to the Council on Social Work Education Annual Meeting: Atlanta, March, 1998.

47 F Field, *The Times*, January 1998.

48 M Wright Edelman, *Families in Peril*, CDF, 1997.

2 Historical concepts of poverty: inclusion or exclusion and US policy design

'What brought the final change of outlook (in the UK) were the economic depression of the 1930s with its tragedy of large-scale unemployment, the increase in medical knowledge and consequent increase in the cost of treatment, and the enforced equality of the war years... The poor were no longer a race apart, to be treated as despised pauper dependents... The welfare of all was a matter of major concern to society as a whole...'

M Bruce, *The Rise of the Welfare State*, 1973, p3

INTRODUCTION

This chapter introduces the basic values that drive social welfare policy in the US. Dependency on others, especially government, is scorned, and self sufficiency rather than mutual support is the goal. The conclusion drawn over thirty years ago by researcher Richard Elman continues to be a valid description of social welfare in the US: 'In the end, our wish to eliminate poverty is matched only by our fervent individualism.'[1] However, the ideal of self-sufficiency contrasts vividly with the reality of suffering brought on by poverty amidst plenty in the US.[2] This contrast is particularly evident in the lives of many children. While working-age adults and some among the elderly enjoy prosperity and increasing social insurance benefits, the income status of children continues to falter.[3] In 1997 two million children were extremely poor in the US, living in families whose income was less than half the level required to be out of poverty.[4] This means that since the reforms in federal welfare policies were enacted, the number of very poor children in the US may be increasing. In considering whether to import welfare-to-work policies from the US, policy makers in the UK must analyze the factors that allow this potential increase in child poverty to be tolerated.

Therefore, comparing the historical development of social welfare policies for children and families in the US to that in the UK, this chapter

- analyzes how recent welfare reforms in the US continue a pattern of promoting self-sufficiency by reducing people's presumed dependency on government assistance;
- describes the selective nature of US policies – they are far less comprehensive than European models, failing for example to provide for universal health care or the family allowances that are standard in other industrialized countries;
- demonstrates the cycles of attention to child poverty in both countries through a time line; and
- suggests a framework for comparative analysis for UK policy makers to use in considering which strategies of welfare reform from the US to adopt.

Reducing dependency rather than alleviating poverty is the primary objective of current US 'welfare' legislation. The assumption is that depending on government support leaves families in poverty, and thus the road out of poverty must be increased self-sufficiency. This assumption overlooks the complex origins of poverty and ignores the fact that in modern societies most families are dependent on government support and services of some kind (such as basic utilities, housing subsidies or income tax deductions, or schools) for their very survival. It also fails to take into account the barriers to gainful employment that many parents face and the low salaries that many jobs pay. After two to five years, if parents do not continue to work, the federal government relinquishes any further responsibility to provide financial support to the family no matter how poor or in need the children are. And how poor are children in the US?

CURRENT LEVEL OF POVERTY FOR CHILDREN IN THE US

Even though the US currently is enjoying the most prosperous economy in the world and is investing some of that wealth into government support for families and children, an estimated 14,500,000 children live in poverty; within that total, 2,000,000 live in abject poverty at less than half the official threshold level set already quite low at $12,980 (approximately £8,655) for a family of three.[5] Thus, 20.5 per cent of the children in the US live in poor families. A Census Bureau report from September, 1998, indicates that 'children represent 40 per cent of the poor, although they are only 26 per cent of the population.'[6] African American, Hispanic or Latino, American Indian, and foreign-born children are disproportionately likely to be living in poverty, an indicator that children are still suffering the effects of racism and discrimination despite the booming economy. Their parents evidently still have less access to educational and employment opportunities available to middle and upper class white parents. Children in different regions of the US suffer disproportionately as well. A study released by the National Center for Children in Poverty at Columbia University on 9 July, 1998, found dramatic variation among the states in the number of children living in poverty. While some states saw decreases, others experienced significant increases from 1992 to 1996 . 'California, Texas, and New York – where nearly half of the poor children live – saw increases of more than 20 per cent.'[7]

Younger children are more likely to be poor. Nearly one in five children under six lives in poverty in the US. Indeed, after accounting for government assistance, the proportion of children lifted out of poverty in the US is just 17 per cent – the lowest increase of any developed country.[8] In Canada, the percentage of children lifted out of poverty after government assistance is over twice as high; in the UK it is four times higher; and in Sweden it is five times higher. While welfare reform efforts are succeeding in some states in lifting some families out of poverty by securing their linkages to employment and the market economy, '[social welfare] benefits lifted 1.1 million fewer children out of extreme poverty in 1997 than in 1995.'[9]

A complex array of factors has led to this neglect of many children's needs in the US. Foremost among them are the fundamental values of the individualistic dominant culture in the US emphasizing 'personal responsibility and work opportunity,' in the words of the federal welfare reform law signed by President Clinton in 1996. The customary approach to child poverty in the US has been and continues to be reliance on individual parents' employment income to secure their children's well-being rather than on financial assistance from the government.

Up until 1935, there was no national entitlement for children in the

US. Only in the middle of the Great Depression, when the need for government assistance to families could no longer be ignored, was the Social Security Act of 1935 passed containing provisions for 'Aid to Dependent Children' (ADC). This programme provided federal money to each state for income maintenance for those children who did not have employed fathers. The intent was to make it possible for mothers to stay home while raising their children, and the assumption was that the programme would be temporary and no longer needed as soon as most fathers could again find jobs. However, ADC and its successor, Aid to Families with Dependent Children (AFDC), became in effect an entitlement to limited federal cash assistance for some very poor families. Benefits varied greatly (as they still do) from state to state, and regulations governing who was eligible were often punitive and mean-spirited as well as means-tested. In addition, the intent of AFDC shifted from encouraging mothers to stay home to one of requiring both parents to seek employment, although during the 1980s AFDC rules actually punished recipients who worked by subtracting their earnings dollar for dollar from their cash grants. And the amount of assistance was deliberately set lower than recipients could make in the lowest paid jobs. Most significantly, in contrast to social security benefits for adults, AFDC grants were rarely adjusted for inflation and thus lost value drastically over time. 'As a result, the median state AFDC payment level declined 47 per cent in real terms from 1970 to 1994.'[10]

The federal reform initiatives in 1996 removed many of the disincentives to work providing some supports such as child care and health insurance during a transitional period, but the new law also eliminated AFDC as an entitlement and replaced it with a time-limited programme aptly entitled Temporary Assistance to Needy Families(TANF).[11] The national policy of the US is that the federal government will not support 'dependency' even when the ultimate effect for some children will be to leave them in poverty. States and families must find other means to meet children's needs without recourse to national entitlements or guaranteed federal support for poor children.

BASIC VALUES DRIVING US SOCIAL WELFARE POLICIES

For those looking to the US for models of effective contemporary social welfare policies, it is essential to understand the values underlying the policies, as well as their deep roots, and their mixed effects. Countries adopting policies such as welfare-to-work without critically examining such initiatives risk unintentionally importing a set of values that are not congruent with their own. This risk may be heightened for European countries because of the many values already shared in common with the US. Indeed, current social welfare policies in the US echo some residual elements in European approaches. Walker's description of European concepts of social welfare with their vestiges of the Victorian era could also be applied to the US model: 'It is true that the market still enjoys pride of place and that other social institutions come a poor second, that individual self reliance is contrasted with dependency on the state, that obligations to work are increasingly enforced, and that tax cuts are given higher priority than improved public services.'[12] However, it is also true that much universally available support remains intact in Europe.

One of the core values of the dominant culture in the US is independence – the freedom of the individual to pursue life and happiness in liberty – a persistent and deep value rising out of the rugged individualism, pioneer spirit, Protestant work ethic, democratic movement and enlightenment philosophies of the 18th century. Still today, dependency is a condition to be avoided at all costs in America, even though, as discussed in Chapter 1, periods of dependence and independence together with the more common human condition of 'interdependence' are all parts of the life cycle. Self reliance is paramount. From Americans of all walks of life, from a variety of backgrounds, and across the generations, one can hear statements such as: 'We are sturdy people, not leaners' and 'It's a disgrace to accept help from someone else to raise your family.' If help is needed, it must be in the form of a 'hand up' not a 'hand out' and then only on a short-term basis to those who are deserving so that people do not become addicted or enslaved to government help.

The American people are justifiably renowned for generous giving and broad community response to those who are victims of catastrophes. Charity and public assistance over a longer term, however, are believed to foster dependency and corrupt the individual's independent spirit, self respect and self esteem. In his essay, 'Self Reliance' published in 1847, Ralph Waldo Emerson gave both philosophical shape and eloquent voice to this value:

> Then, again, do not tell me, as a good man did today, of my obligation to
> put all poor men in good situations. Are they my poor? I tell thee, thou

foolish philanthropist, that I grudge the dollar, the dime, the cent I give to such men as do not belong to me and to whom I do not belong. There is a class of persons to whom by all spiritual affinity I am bought and sold; for them I will go to prison, if need be: but not your miscellaneous popular charities; the education at college of fools; the building of meeting-houses to the vain end to which many now stand; alms to sots; and the thousand fold Relief Societies – though I confess with shame I sometimes succumb and give the dollar, it is a wicked dollar which by and by I shall have the manhood to withhold.[13]

Such sentiments have profound meaning for the development of any system of social inclusion. A general distrust of the benefit of giving help to those in need persists in the US today. Social exclusion – meaning the denial of rights to societal support – is not part of the public discourse about poverty. Lack of material resources or income (poverty) is seen as a condition separate from issues related to human rights, and the link between being poor and being shut out of integration with society is not visible to many. Compared to other democratic countries, many people in America hold judgmental beliefs and attitudes towards those who are poor if they are perceived as separate, not included in the 'mainstream' of working society; Emerson's emphasis in 'Are they my poor?' is still representative.

HISTORICAL DEVELOPMENT OF SOCIAL WELFARE POLICIES FOR CHILDREN AND FAMILIES IN THE US

A few years after Emerson's essay, the famous Pierce Veto of 1854 set back government intervention in social funding in the US, at least until the New Deal of the 1930s. During the 1840s there had been extensive discussion concerning federal funding of services for the mentally ill. President Pierce firmly opposed this idea. Dorothea Dix, the campaigner for improved facilities and treatment for mentally ill patients, introduced a bill for Congress in the year following 'Self Reliance' to appropriate ten million acres to states to help provide for the construction and maintenance of mental hospitals. Historian Walter Trattner writes that

> Numerous clergymen, prominent citizens, newspapers, public and private organizations, including the Association of Medical Superintendents for the Insane, and some government officials wrote or

acted in support of the measure. Still the bill was not acted upon, for most congressmen were more interested in using the remaining public domain for their own and for land speculators' purposes than for the mentally ill.[14]

Despite this set back, Dorothea Dix lobbied both the House and Senate, and Congress eventually passed the bill in 1854, only to have it vetoed by President Pierce in terms that echo down the years:

> If Congress has the power to make provision for the indigent insane,…it has the same power for the indigent who are not insane…I cannot find any authority in the Constitution for making the Federal Government the great almoner of public charity throughout the United States…[To do so] would be contrary to the letter and spirit of the Constitution, and subversive of the whole theory upon which the union of these states is founded.[15]

These attitudes which include some 'like us' (hard working) while excluding 'others' (different, indigent, insane, loafing) manifest themselves in the historical development of welfare policies in the US (see figure 2.1, p39). Historically and currently, if people are in poverty through no evident fault of their own, because of disability or age, for example, they deserve to be included in 'our poor.' People are categorized as 'undeserving' or 'unworthy' of help, however, if they are perceived to be poor because of personal frailties such as laziness, inebriation or lack of thrift. Although children are usually seen as 'deserving,' children whose parents are categorized as 'undeserving' are often excluded from the embrace of the community's social welfare even though they are obviously not 'at fault.'

Residual (short-term, means-tested) approaches to welfare are thus the norm; for example food stamp programs, medical coverage for people receiving assistance, and public housing assistance. The few universal programmes such as public education suffer constant retrenchments, budget cuts and political attacks. At the National Conference on Charity and Corrections in 1890, Josephine Shaw Lowell, leader among the charity organization societies in the US, argued against the use of public tax revenue to give financial assistance to people in their own homes. She believed that the more government dispersed relief, the worse off people were. 'There can be no question that there is an inverse ratio between the welfare of the mass of the people and the distribution of relief.' She then illustrated her argument with a telling allegory against proposals to invest more universal public funding in meeting people's basic needs. It illustrates the depth of American's revulsion toward dependency and pre-figures the rise of attention to the needs and perceptions of the middle class that is evoked by the Clinton administration today. (It is worthwhile to note that she changed her mind and social Darwinist leanings after the devastation wrought by the economic depression later in the decade made clear that the causes of poverty were structural and required government responses. She devoted much of her subsequent work to advocating for single young women and mothers.)

In her allegory, residents in the Valley of Industry lived by pumping water from an aquifer beneath them to a reservoir above on the Hill of Prosperity. Each household received an ample supply of water from the reservoir by way of pipes leading to each house, 'each man receiving what he himself pumped up.' In time, some residents of the valley moved up the Hill and began to tap the reservoir for their own use. Despite having to pump harder to keep the reservoir full, the workers did not complain. Meanwhile, people on the Hill discovered another valley – the Valley of Idleness – where people 'were living in abject misery, with no water and apparently no means of getting any.' Feeling sorry for the 'poor things,' the people on the Hill started a pipe directing water from the reservoir to the Valley of Idleness. Soon, some tired, weak, or lazy pumpers in the Valley of Industry heard about the 'free water' in the other valley and moved there. (Lowell reminds us that the water 'was not free at all; for the Valley of Industry people paid for it with their blood and muscle.') This necessitated that the people on the Hill build more pipes, divert more water, forcing the few people left in the Valley of Industry to pump harder as more lazy people left. However, the people on the Hill grew perplexed, as 'the children born in the Valley of Idleness did not even know there was a Valley of Industry or any pumps or any pumpers or any reservoir; they thought the water grew in pipes and ran out because it was its nature to.' Lowell wants her listeners to pay attention to how children on relief might become accustomed to and dependent upon public help, not learning that deserving adults must work to become self-sufficient.

Thus, as we will see in Chapter 3, US social welfare approaches including the current insistence on moving parents from welfare to work imply that it is more important that children learn that hard work can bring them something approaching well-being than it is for children to have their needs met. In many states (Wisconsin, for example), a popular slogan is: 'The best welfare programme is a job.' Others believe, as is stated by welfare officials in Minnesota, that 'work must pay' – that is, that if parents are working, the family should not be poor. Nevertheless, work and learning to get to work regularly and on time are seen as pre-eminent, regardless of any structural problems that might exist.

The perception that most people are poor because they made themselves poor, that they would not be in poverty if they didn't want to be, that opportunities for self reliance abound, has been maintained tenaciously. The myth persists that dependence is tantamount to mortal sin and damnable irresponsibility. To be included in the fabric of community as deserving of help, people paradoxically must show how they are independent of community support. Welfare agencies in the US often now go by such titles as the 'Training and Employment Assistance Program,' and parents who use welfare services are called 'job seekers.' One of the priority goals of a typical such agency is 'giving special emphasis to reversing the pervasive welfare culture which puts the delivery of public financial assistance before expectations of personal responsibility.'[16] Caseworkers are urged on with slogans like: 'A job is the first step out of poverty,' 'only work works,' 'any job is better than no job,' and 'a reduction in welfare dependents is better than total welfare dependence.'[17] Ironically, the federal government has recently had to take the extraordinary step of advertising for eligible individuals to take advantage of food stamps and medical assistance. 'The fear is that local governments may be blocking access to food stamps and Medicaid as they persuade people to give up the dole, snatching a valuable crutch from welfare mothers hobbling toward self-reliance.'[18]

In other countries, such as the UK, government assistance is not seen so much as a 'crutch' but rather an entitlement deserved by every citizen to have basic needs met. What, then, are some differences in the history and current reality of 'welfare' between the US and the UK? Both countries have espoused the concept of a 'safety net' for those experiencing poverty, a net through which none should fall. The policies of the 'New Deal' in the US of the 1930s and the 'Welfare State' in the UK of the 1940s most clearly represent this net. Following the Second World War, children's well-being was a priority with politicians in the UK[19] However, in view of the persistence of poverty – particularly for children – in both countries and despite the positive shifts that have occurred for example in infant mortality and literacy, it is easy for critics to claim that the net has failed.

Figure 2.1 compares chronological landmarks in social welfare policy initiatives in the US with those in the UK. While marking some important expansions of government responsibility for the welfare of children, it also shows how reluctant US policy makers have been to move to the universal welfare provisions common in Europe, especially for children who live in poor families.

In summary, then, abhorrence of dependency in the US leads some influential politicians and other policy makers to conclude, in the face of mounting evidence to the contrary, that if there are fewer mothers dependent on welfare benefits (as indicated by the reduction that many states are currently experiencing in the number of cases on public assistance), then there must be fewer mothers and children who are poor. If families are not being helped by government, they must either be self sufficient (that is, deserving, hard working, responsible, earning their keep, independent Americans) or derelict, neglectful parents whose hard-up kids are 'at risk' (unworthy and a drain on society). Ask many Americans their visual image of families in this latter category, and if honest they will describe a family with darker skin, speaking an English different from their own, and whose culture, tradition and values are vaguely 'un-American.' The stereotype of the 'Welfare Queen' – sitting at home, staring blankly at the TV, addicted to drugs, and neglecting her children whose many fathers are nowhere to be found – is prevalent and robust.

A FRAMEWORK FOR CROSS-NATIONAL COMPARISONS

When examining claims of success in welfare reform in the US, policy makers in the UK will find it useful to keep in mind the core values and historical development underlying social welfare policies for families and children living in poverty that we have outlined in this chapter. The framework in figure 2.2 is suggested for comparing US strategies with others.

If we apply this framework to a comparison of US and UK social welfare policies for meeting the needs of poor families, we can describe the US approach as ambivalent and fragmented, even half-hearted and begrudging, not wanting to see children starve or be homeless, but very worried about fostering dependency or discouraging work. Social welfare programmes may temporarily shore up family income, but not nearly to the point that families could live on it. 'Less eligibility' – the old poor law concept that public financial aid to families should be lower than the lowest paid worker could earn – still governs policies for financial assistance. Food stamps and other food supplements such as those provided by the Women, Infant, and Children (WIC) Program, provide some basic supplies. Some basic health care may be available in the US at low cost or free, but even basic public health measures such as immunizations are not guaranteed and free to all children as they are in every other industrialized country. Some poor families may live in partially subsidized housing, but increasing numbers are homeless, living in shelters, crammed into apartments with other families or living in their cars. Families are expected to use their grants to purchase clothes and other necessities when rent or child care expenses can easily consume most of the grant. Although public transport, if available, can be inexpensive, and libraries are open and free for public use in most communities, there is little spare money in a typical public assistance grant for transport or entertainment.

One of the few universal programmes is the public school system; educational needs are addressed in the US in pre-school, elementary and high school, but facilities are of mixed quality. In what Jonathan Kozol calls 'savage inequalities,' children from poor families often have no choice other than to attend dilapidated and understaffed schools in dangerous neighbourhoods.[21] Police protection is sometimes not forthcoming for children in poorer communities. Poor children with emotional or mental health needs are disproportionately served by the public child protection and juvenile correction systems, while children from middle class homes with similar needs are more likely to be served by the private mental health system.

It is clear, therefore, that most social welfare programmes used by poor families in the US are residual (see p41, figure 2.2). Federal guarantees of assistance to poor families first enacted in the US during the 1930s and strengthened in the 60s and 70s have been repealed. The responsibility for meeting the needs of poor people has been 'devolved' to the states and local government authorities. But the resources available to states and localities vary considerably and the chances of a child's needs being met therefore also vary according to where he or she happens to live. The observation that government support for services to the poor tends to increase in hard times (some say as a way to pacify the poor) but diminish in times of prosperity appears accurate. There is an opportunity, though, to take advantage of the differences between the way each state has chosen to implement the current welfare-to-work policies. For example, Minnesota and Wisconsin have taken divergent paths and present alternative strategies for analysis and consideration by policy makers in the UK. Programmes in both of

FIGURE 2.1: **Comparison of Chronological Landmarks in Development of Social Welfare Policies**

For Children in Families Living in Poverty

	In the US	In the UK
1906		School meals
1909	White House Conference on Dependent Children Initiates progressive era reforms that lead to establishment of the federal Children's Bureau, the first major endorsement by the national government of public aid to women and dependent children.	War budget: warfare on poverty.
1919		Council housing: Homes Fit for Heroes
1934		Unemployment Assistance Board Act.
1935	Title 4 of the Social Security Act: ADC Provides federal matching funds to augment states' mother's pensions by providing Aid to Dependent Children (ADC) who are deprived of parental support; the goal is to support mothers who were widowed or in homes without bread winners to stay home and raise their children; means-tested and extreme variation among states in the level of aid.	
1945		Family Allowances
1948		'Appointed day' for implementation of National Assistance Act; National Insurance Act; National Health Service Act; and Children Act.
1950	ADC changed to AFDC Additional allowance for 'caretaker' grants to parent as well as to dependent children.	
1962	Social Service Amendments to AFDC Combine financial and social services relying more on counselling and case work to reinforce the work ethic of parents rather than on cash assistance; do provide some additional funds to families and attempt to standardize grant levels and eligibility across the states; broaden coverage to families	

	with unemployed parents; permit states to require unemployed parents to participate in community work and training programs as a condition for eligibility.	
1966		Ministry of Social Security Act.
1967	WIN Work Incentive Program mandates AFDC recipients to participate in education and training activities for work.	
1971		Family Income Supplement.
1972	SSI Supplemental Security Income – first guaranteed annual income for elderly, blind, disabled, including eligible children.	
1980		Social Security Act rules of entitlement for extras formerly available on discretionary basis.
1986		Social Security Act Social Fund replaces 1980 entitlements.
1988	Family Support Act Strict work requirements.	
1991		Child Support Act
1994		Social Security (Incapacity for work) Act
1995		Jobseekers Act
1996	Personal Responsibility and Work Opportunity Act	
1999	Welfare Reform & Pensions Act	

these states are undergoing rigorous study and the results are revealing the strengths and limitations of each as they affect children in those states. Outcomes could indicate problems with the whole welfare reform effort; a recent compilation of over 30 state and local studies cites the hardships many families are encountering as parents take extremely low paying jobs. More government, community, and employer services will be needed to help families meet children's needs. For example, Georgia has found that in its WorkFirst programme only 14.2 per cent of former welfare recipients were earning more than

---

FIGURE 2.2: **Framework for Analysis of Social Welfare Policies** [20]

---

1. Examine the general approach to meeting human needs that is currently in place in the country. Which needs have been identified as the responsibility of social welfare programmes and which have not?

2. Determine if the social welfare policies and programmes are universal or selective, and institutional or residual (or a combination). Into which of these two columns of descriptive terms would most of the social welfare programs and services fall? Remember to include those fiscal support programmes such as tax relief benefits or 'corporate welfare'.

Social Insurance	or	Social Assistance
Preventive	or	Rehabilitative
Comprehensive	or	Limited by Categories
Public Sector, National	or	Private Sector, or local government
Rights and Justice	or	Charity

3. Analyze the historical context of the needs that social welfare policies and programmes seek to address, of the barriers or catalysts to government responses, and of the factors that influence identification of a particular need in the first place.

4. Generate a list of plausible alternatives to meet the human needs that are intended to be addressed by existing social welfare policies and programmes, focusing on strengths and resources to build upon. The social welfare programmes of other countries are a fruitful source for alternative approaches.

5. Analyze the anticipated benefits and drawbacks of each alternative and the potential unintended outcomes, both negative and positive.

6. Compare these benefits and drawbacks to the outcomes of social welfare policies and programmes currently in place.

7. If appropriate and in partnership with community members, propose an alternative social welfare policy and prepare to evaluate its effects if implemented.

---

minimum wage.[22] A recent report of preliminary studies on how families are doing during welfare reform found that

> Some former recipients appear to be faring better off welfare. Work supports and wage supplements are making it easier for some parents to work, and evaluations suggest that a few especially supportive programs are both helping families go to work and lifting them out of poverty. These successes deserve much attention and replication.

But less-well known findings suggest another side of the picture: an increase in extreme childhood poverty nation wide; proliferation of inadequately-paid employment; and signs of rising hardship for many families leaving welfare. Policy and implementation failures at the local, state and federal level often appear to contribute to these hardships.[23]

This chapter has focused on how the problem of children living in poverty is defined in the US as a function of dependency rather than poverty. Countries who have focused on meeting children's needs have turned to such measures as family allowances or guaranteed minimum incomes for families and have been less concerned that this assistance will foster dependency. Policy makers could reasonably introduce or augment a system of family allowances as an alternative to current welfare reform initiatives that rely on parents finding and maintaining employment and hoping that their work pays enough and carries adequate benefits (for example, health insurance) to meet their children's needs. The likelihood of such a proposal reaching implementation in the US is slim because of the core values of self reliance and distrust of government assistance, but many European countries already have family allowances in place. Fine-tuning and bolstering that kind of government responsibility for the well-being of children will hold more promise than the welfare-to-work strategies popular in the US, as we will see in Chapter 3.

NOTES

1 R M Elman, *The Poorhouse State: The American Way of Life on Public Assistance*, Dell, 1966.
2 Children's Defense Fund. *The State of America's Children: A report for the Children's Defense Fund*, Beacon Press, 1998.
3 N M Ozawa, The Economic Well-Being of Elderly People and Children in a Changing Society, *Social Work*, 44 (1), 1999.
4 Children's Defense Fund & National Coalition for the Homeless. *Welfare to What: Early Findings on Family Hardship and Well-Being*, Washington, DC, November, 1998.
5 A Sherman, *Poverty Matters: The Cost of Child Poverty in America*. Children's Defense Fund, 1997. See also *Welfare to What*, (note 4).
6 'Blacks, Hispanics Lead Drop in Poverty Rate', Minneapolis *Star Tribune*, 25 September, 1998.
7 'Number of Children in Poverty is up 12 Per cent, Study Says', Minneapolis *Star Tribune*, 10 July, 1998.
8 L Rainwater & T M Smeeding, 'Doing Poorly: The Real Income of American Children in a Comparative Perspective', *Working Paper No. 127, Luxemburg Income Study*. Maxwell School of Citizenship and Public Affairs, 1995.

9 *Welfare to What*, (note 4), p52. The number of children living in families with income less than half the poverty level ($6,401 per year for a family of three) increased by 400,000.

10 Ozawa, (note 3), citing the US House of Representatives Committee on Ways and Means, *1994 Overview of Entitlement Programs*, 1994.

11 'Under the previous welfare law, public assistance was an entitlement for all families that met certain income eligibility guidelines. The new law places a 60-month lifetime limit on welfare receipt. States have latitude to create even stricter time limits or to exempt some families from the 60 month limit.' M Zaslow, K Tout, C Botsko & K Moore, *Welfare Reform and Children: Potential Implications*, The Urban Institute, 1998.

12 R Walker 'Poverty and Social Exclusion in Europe' in A Walker and C Walker (eds), *Britain Divided: The Growth of Social Exclusion in the 1980s and 1990s*, CPAG, 1997.

13 R W Emerson, 'Self Reliance', *The Oxford Authors: Ralph Waldo Emerson*, (Edited by Richard Poirier) Oxford University Press, 1990.

14 W Trattner, *From the Poor Law to the Welfare State: A History of Social Welfare in America*, (5th Edition), Free Press.

15 Trattner (note 14), 1994, quoting Pierce's veto message.

16 Minnesota Department of Training and Employment Assistance. *TEA Times*, November 1998.

17 Minnesota Department of Training and Employment Assistance. *TEA Times*, September, 1998.

18 R L Swarns, 'In an odd turn, federal officials are pushing food stamps, Medicaid.' Minneapolis *Star Tribune*, 29 November 1998.

19 'Beveridge had made family allowances one of the three assumptions of his report, and they were accepted by the coalition government…By a free vote the Commons decided that the allowances should be paid to the mother. The first payments were made in August 1946. From the Family Allowances Act, 1945: 1. Subject to the provisions of this Act, there shall be paid by the Minister, out of moneys provided by Parliament, for every family which includes two or more children and the for the benefit of the family as a whole, an allowance in respect of each child in the family other than the eldest at the rate of five shillings a week…' M Bruce, *The Rise of the Welfare State*, Weidenfeld and Nicolson, 1973.

20 C S Ramanathan & R J Link, *All Our Futures: Principles and Resources for Social Work Practice in a Global Era*. Brooks/Cole.

21 J Kozol, *Savage Inequalities: Children in America's Schools*, Crown, 1991.

22 Children's Defense Fund. 'After Welfare, Many Families Fare Worse' News Release, 2 December 1998; http://www.2.state.ga.us/BROC/peach/html

23 *Welfare to What*, (note 4).

3 Welfare to work: Is it workable?

'The female rate of involuntary part-time work is 44 per cent greater than that for men [in the US]...one fifth of families headed by part-time workers are in poverty...Single mothers do not turn to welfare because they are pathologically dependent on handouts or reluctant to work – they do so because they cannot get jobs that pay better...'
J Handler, *We the Poor People*, 1995, p. 53

US welfare policy is defined in many states by an emphasis on getting back to work. For example, Minnesota's legislative summary refers to 'A tough but fair solution to welfare dependency...Minnesota's 1997 Welfare Reform Law valuing work, responsibility and families'.[1] The focus of this legislation is individual responsibility, in an atmosphere where people seeking income maintenance are considered not to value employment since they have been dependent on the state and such dependency means that they are in need of tough lessons. The policy makes quite clear who is responsible for poverty: the people in poverty themselves, men, women and children, not the state, not the government, not employers, not society as a whole. Also clear is the message that support is time limited, with a maximum of five year's cash assistance in a lifetime. The five year clock started ticking in most states in 1997, and no federal plans have yet been identified for children's survival needs when their parents start reaching their limits in 2002. However, at the time of writing in early 2000, some states are relenting and considering the needs for extended counselling and support services and for renewed funding to help families in the transition to work. The irony for many states is that in the rush to remove people from welfare rolls, the inadequacy of salaries for part-time and low skilled jobs to lift people out of poverty, was underestimated. Now there is growing unease that 2002 approaches with little cover for destitute children, while the welfare coffers of many states stand full:

> Governor Jesse Ventura announced a new $173 million sortie in Minnesota's war on poverty...A sharp reduction in the state's welfare rolls has left Minnesota with a big surplus in its federal welfare account. That balance is expected to reach $223 million by 2003, or nearly enough to fund the state's welfare programme for a year...Minnesota's version of the national welfare-to-work experiment has posted several achievements. The number of welfare recipients holding jobs has nearly doubled since 1997, and the number of families receiving public assistance has fallen sharply. As of last July, however, fully 36 per cent of welfare recipients were not working.[2]

While the central theme of US Welfare Reform is work, we now discuss the narrowness of a definition of poverty which blames the individual as dependent rather than looks at the many layers of poverty. These layers include structural unemployment (for example, unemployment beyond individual control, systemic and large scale, as a result of plant closings or regional depression where groups of people are suddenly laid off); lack of access to work above the minimum wage; mismatch between qualifications and opportunities; geographic isolation; availability of childcare; and varying access to health benefits. Added to these practical factors is the ethical question of who is deemed 'dependent' and how it has come to be such a stigma. All adults are, from time to time, dependent on others, for example when pregnant and in labour, when sick, disabled, elderly; and none of us is wholly independent. Rather in a complex global society we are interdependent. Therefore, we ask 'Is justice just jobs?' and wonder whether the objective is to get people off the 'welfare rolls' into the workplace regardless of their future prospects or improved living standards. The emphasis in this chapter is the implementation of income maintenance policy in the US and its unintended consequences.

In an era of 'downsizing' and technological advances leading to less need for menial human tasks, the nature of employment is changing drastically and rapidly; but how realistically is this being analyzed in terms of 'job seeking'? The European Social Chapter discusses the value of work in the home (ie. for parents who choose to stay in the home with children under five) and proposes that such 'work' be included in definitions of employment.[3] These ideas have not gained currency in the US or UK despite recognition of shifting labour needs. There are successful projects supporting former welfare recipients in the USA, and these will be highlighted so that we can identify policies to promote as well as those to avoid.

In their summary of the US Welfare Reform Bill, Bread for the World remind their readers that 'the US child poverty rate is 20.8 per cent – three times the average of other industrial countries...and the welfare bill is likely to push an additional 2.6 million people – including 1.1 million children – into poverty'[4] In their list of goals for state policy and advocacy the group includes the following:

- ensuring that all eligible people, particularly children, will receive assistance;
- providing adequate benefits; and
- providing family-sustaining jobs.

The third item, sustaining and sustainable jobs, is the particular concern of this chapter. Many states in the US, including Wisconsin, have claimed 'success' in their welfare changes because people have been dropped from their rolls and have re-entered the workforce or dropped from sight. However, there are critical issues in terms of the quality of jobs available for recent welfare recipients and the likelihood of their being able to enter a career which will take them permanently out of poverty. A recent report by the Institute for Wisconsin's future found, for example, that while the number of people on welfare decreased by 67 per cent, the number of people in poverty dropped by only 11.8 per cent. As emphasized by Bread for the World, 'requiring people to work means that states must create jobs that pay a livable wage and do not displace present workers. Programmes should eliminate barriers to employment and provide child care, transportation, education and training, and other services that will make participation feasible.'

While recognizing that employment is not the complete picture in relation to income maintenance and tackling poverty, in this chapter we nevertheless consider the central focus of the current US welfare reforms: getting people to work. To fulfil this plan the following questions will be examined.

- Who are the able-bodied people who fail to work?
- What keeps them out of employment?
- Are jobs available that match the skills of people needing them?
- What education opportunities are provided in current policy?

• What are the prospects for children when work comes first: family-friendly employers and childcare?

WHO ARE THE ABLE-BODIED WHO FAIL TO WORK?

This question elicits a complex mixture of relative values and moral confusion. For example, it is well documented in relation to child poverty that it is economically hazardous for parents, mostly women, to raise children under five alone. Being a lone or single parent is hazardous because if parents stay at home to care for their children themselves, they have no access to income; or, if employed, they are likely to be in part-time or low-paid employment. Unlike the situation in Scandinavia and Italy, where the emphasis is on child allowance, family services, child care provision and the overall well-being of the child, the US has systematically simplified the equation in relation to families with young children.[5] Parents must work. Getting to work is not so simple, however. When there are children under three in a family they need constant attention; parents can care for children or pay childminders. When someone is employed for this task, it is considered work; when we care for our own child it is also work, but not classified as such.

Although research informs us that children flourish in secure, familiar, structured, nurturing surroundings, in the US these data are still not reflected in legislative initiatives.[6] The National Commission on Children in the US is quite critical of the requirements of the Welfare Reform policies which require women to seek work twelve weeks after childbirth:

> The first years of life are a period of great vulnerability and opportunity. Infants and toddlers are wholly dependent on their parents (and other caregivers) to meet their basic needs. Without adequate nutrition and nurturing to fuel their rapid development, many children suffer delayed or stunted growth, impaired intellectual development, unresponsiveness, and low resistance to infection.[7]

Frequently, for welfare 'moms' returning to work, the primary concern is child care, transport and caring for their children when they are sick (testimony of workers involved with young children, such as the Southside Family Nurturing Center, Focus Groups, March 1999).[8] Therefore, one response to the question 'who are the able-bodied who fail to work,' is that most are in fact working when we acknowledge the hard, rewarding, constant 'work' of child raising. The majority of welfare applicants in the US are lone mothers with children; when we reframe parents' childcare as work, the majority of able-bodied recipients become workers. The issue then becomes to what age should care of children be considered work – infants up to the age of three or pre-school children up to five years old? Currently, parents who are poor often have no choice except to work outside their homes and arrange child care for their children. Compared with the wide condemnation of mothers on welfare who are not 'working' outside their homes, there is a remarkable absence of comment in the US on middle and upper income families where mothers (and some fathers) choose to stay at home.

It is time to move away from the judgements and stereotypes of people being lazy and dependent. While a small majority may have lost the energy to participate in the employment market, unemployment is not something anyone envies. Unemployment combined with inadequate income causes self esteem to plummet, it becomes a vicious circle of self doubt, failure begetting depression, begetting inactivity, sometimes leading to drug addiction or suicide.[9] Poverty is something we rarely choose. It is draining, exhausting, and as Kotlowitz has vividly shown, sucks away at the vitality of children's lives.[10] One recommendation to be discussed in our concluding chapter is the inclusion of adequate parental child care when calculating benefits, either through increased children's allowance or integrated income tax credit. This also assumes that we no longer stigmatize people without formal employment and include them as part of the fabric of society in the way wealthier people have already coined the term 'working in the home.'

A challenge for 'welfare' policy makers in the US and UK would be to live for a month on the benefit to which we would be entitled if out of official work, without the support of our clubs, workplaces and social network. In his article 'Get the rich off the dole', Peter Peterson, a Republican who served as Secretary of Commerce in the US, questions the ready response that the elderly are more needy and deserving of social security than children; are some of them 'able-bodied,' should they be receiving a lion's share of benefits?

> If a couple has a retirement income of more than $32,000, half of their social security income is taxed (in 1988)…I say when a person hits somewhere between $40,000 and $100,000 a year, tax it 100 per

cent…My father told me that kids should do better than their parents. We now have a situation where our young workers have had a decline in real income after taxes, where a child is six times more likely to be in poverty than the elderly.[11]

The situation has worsened in the past ten years to the extent that 50 per cent of Black children are living in poverty.[12] Furthermore, it is important to note that for Europe the term 'social security' refers to the life span approach to income maintenance, while in the US it applies only to the category of the elderly. Ten years ago Peterson and colleagues focused on the contradiction of limiting universal concepts of 'social security' only to the elderly, when all our futures depend on a social environment and arrangements by central governments where children can thrive.

The final and most stark fact about who is 'on welfare' is the overwhelming number of children, who do not represent 'able-bodied adults' but who benefit or suffer the opportunities and deficits of income maintenance policy:

FIGURE 3.1: **Who's on welfare**		1997 US
7,770,000.	2,339,000.	1,138,000.
CHILDREN	lone parents	married parents

Source: Minnesota Dept. of Human Services, quoted in the Star Tribune, 30 August 1998, A25.

This table is a reminder of who will suffer in 2002. There can be no understatement of the impact on children of Welfare Reform.[13]

WHAT KEEPS THE POOR OUT OF EMPLOYMENT?

The answer to 'what keeps welfare recipients out of employment' is many layered. When the definition of employment is re-framed to include parenting, large numbers of recipients become included among those considered able-bodied and working, but they, nonetheless, remain in poverty. Cash grants to families on welfare in the US are substantially below the federally set poverty line. Thus, there can be a financial incentive for parents to seek employment outside the home. There are, however, several deterrents to seeking employment: moving into the workplace can mean losing real income, health coverage, childcare or housing; available jobs may not improve living conditions because they are concentrated in the lowest paid and part-time sector; employment at the lowest paid end of the market is often insecure; there is frequently a mismatch between qualifications and opportunities and a lack of financial support for time spent by adults in education.[14]

FIGURE 3.2: **Perceived Barriers from Welfare to Work**

Group 1	Group 2	Group 3
Welfare Participants	County Workers	Employment Service Provider
wages	motivation	transportation
job availability	transportation	job skills
health insurance	job skills	soft skills*
education	soft skills*	mental health
work experience	substance abuse	motivation
transportation	care providers	care providers
job skills	housing	housing
child care availability	English-speaking skills	substance abuse
health issues	domestic issues	physical health
child care costs	lack of jobs	domestic issues

Note. Barriers listed from the top as most perceived barrier in descending order.
Group 1 = welfare participants (n = 265).
Group 2 = county financial workers (n = 74).
Group 3 = employment service providers (n = 56).
*Note. Soft Skills – work behaviors, attitudes, motivation, and ability to interact with others.
(with permission: Patrick Pischke, MSW)

A Minnesota researcher, Patrick Pischke, identifies the different perceptions of welfare recipients, administrators and employers and introduces figure 3.2 as follows:

> Recent studies conducted by the Minnesota Department of Human Services indicate various perceptions of barriers Minnesota welfare

recipients encounter as they leave public assistance and go into the mainstream employment sector. Figure 3.2 displays the findings of three different perspectives of perceived barriers to employment faced by Minnesota welfare recipients involved with the Minnesota Family Investment Program (MFIP). The implications of these studies support the complexity involved with designing and implementing effective welfare-to-work (workfare) programmes.

It is noteworthy in figure 3.2 that welfare participants list adequate wages and job availability first among many practical barriers. Neither county social workers not employers list wages as a barrier, but they do identify motivation as an issue. Welfare participants do not judge themselves to be without motivation – others do that for them.

In the UK it has been well documented that the unemployed jobseeker can better improve his or her living standards, not by seeking employment at minimum wage, but by seeking long-term sickness and disability allowance. Similarly, in the US, people previously receiving Aid to Families with Dependent Children were likely to be worse off in low-paid work since they lost benefits such as medicaid. Political rhetoric captures public attention by focusing on negative judgements of poor people as dependent, morally deficient and fraudulent, when in truth for any person trying to survive on substandard wages in the US or UK, life is a struggle. As stated by Hutton: 'Benefits in the UK are the most cheapskate and meanest in Europe... the choice to live on benefit is unimaginably tough.'[15] Similarly, Gill of the Fulford Family Centre has documented the lives of women living with children under five as a constant juggling act between light, heat, food, transport and nappies.[16] A scan of the variety of grants available from state to state in the US demonstrates the varying rates of support and destitution. Long and Clark, in their study of block grants and state funding choices and their implications', reveal that although Welfare Reform provides greater funding for child care, this is undermined by the choices and variety in take-up of block grants, state to state.[17]

In essence, it is not laziness or frail dependence that keeps the majority of people, often women, out of work, but a lack of financial and practical gain towards family survival compounded by a lack of educational qualifications. In instances, such as the Minnesota Family Investment Program (MFIP) where Welfare Reform measures are accompanied by state support for childcare, health and housing, the future can (with adequate employer supports) look bright for people with qualifications. Predictably, these supports are more costly than simply dropping people from the rolls and have not, therefore, been recognized politically as reaching the levels of 'success' that have been claimed in states such as Wisconsin, which points to reduced rolls and reduced costs in the short term.

Furthermore, in comparing the US with other industrialized countries, Rainwater has emphasized the irony of claiming success through the narrow prism of 'back to work.' Her research states 'although the US has high proportions of families in work, it has the largest earning differentials, the lowest social transfers, and the highest poverty rates.'[18] Low-paying, service-sector jobs are the most readily available to people re-entering the workforce with low educational qualifications, but the most fragile, especially in terms of layoff and the 'last in, first out' management mentality. Also, these jobs do not lead to career advancement or to optimistic economic futures for the children of parents taking this path. Rainwater is explicit: 'poverty rates are dependent on the labour market.' Illustrating this point, Handler offers these stark figures:

- more than 25 per cent of women work part-time without long term benefits;
- the female rate of involuntary part-time work is 44 per cent greater than that for men; and
- one fifth of families headed by part-time workers are in poverty. [19]

The situation is no better in the UK. The current Labour Government published the 'Welfare Reform Focus Files' in March 1998 which included the following information.

- 2.8 million children in the UK are now living in workless households – a threefold increase on 1979.
- For women in workless households the most important reason is because they are a lone parent. In 1996, 31 per cent of women in workless households were lone parents, compared with 17 per cent in 1979.
- Children in workless households are most commonly found in lone parent families.
- 49 per cent of non-working lone parents in 1994 in the UK had no qualifications.[20]

Thus, since many of the able-bodied people who are failing to work are women with children, it would seem reasonable to suppose that what keeps them out of employment has been the need to care for dependents, to have adequate childcare, health benefits and transport.

These conditions exist even before the question of availability of jobs, matching of skills and education are considered.

ARE JOBS AVAILABLE THAT MATCH THE SKILLS OF PEOPLE NEEDING THEM?

According to the UK Focus Files, as in the US, the 'overwhelming majority of the 1.7 million lone parents are lone mothers'. More worrying is the information that not only are lone mothers with children very short of qualifications for employment, the gap is

---

FIGURE 3.3: **Minnesota Case Studies: Nils Dybvig (composite case studies, confidentiality of names maintained)**

Background summary

In January 1998, the state of Minnesota began a new welfare programme called the Minnesota Family Investment Program (MFIP). This programme was created in response to federal welfare reform and has taken the place of Aid to Families with Dependent Children (AFDC) in Minnesota. Under the new programme most adult assistance recipients must meet with job counsellors to draw up an employment plan. They are required to spend thirty hours per week searching for full-time work and document their time on a job search calendar. MFIP recipients who are job seeking as well as those who find jobs are provided with sliding-fee child care assistance and medical insurance.

MFIP recipients who do not comply with job search requirements may be sanctioned. The first instance of non-compliance results in a 10 per cent reduction of the welfare grant, and child care assistance is withdrawn. Subsequent sanctions reduce the grant by 30 per cent and the recipient's rent is deducted first and paid directly to their landowner. This is meant to ensure that the recipient does not become homeless due to a sanction, but it also often results in reducing the grant to almost nothing.

The Case of ANNE

Anne, a 25-year-old mother of two daughters, aged 2 and 4, has received public assistance since her divorce two years ago. Anne was enthusiastic during her initial meeting with her job counsellor and told her counsellor she was looking forward to returning to work. Before the advent of MFIP Anne had tried to return to work several times but without paid child care she could not afford to work. Since Anne had some secretarial experience her job counsellor suggested that Anne enrol in a four-week computer class to update her office skills. The job counsellor assisted Anne in signing-up to be reimbursed for child care during her job search.

After completing the computer training Anne quickly found a part-time job processing checks for a bank. Her job counsellor referred Anne to a church programme that gives MFIP recipients clothes for a professional wardrobe. Anne continued to receive a portion of her MFIP grant because her earned income did not exceed the MFIP guidelines. The combination of wages and reduced MFIP grant are significantly greater than Anne's MFIP grant with no earnings. In addition, her child care costs are paid by the state. Anne was thrilled with her new position and told her job counsellor she was relieved to be back in the work force. After a few months, Anne accepted the offer of a full-time position at the bank and her earned income was now sufficient to move her off MFIP assistance. At this level of earnings Anne pays a small monthly co-payment for child care and her full medical insurance is provided by the state. Child care assistance and medical insurance are guaranteed for one year after Anne moves off the MFIP grant.

The Case of BETTY

Betty is a single 45-year-old mother of five children, ages 6 to 18, who has received public assistance for the last 14 years. She graduated from high school but reads and writes with difficulty. With some direction from her job counsellor, Betty applied to be a cashier at a grocery store and was hired to work twenty hours per week. Due to her limited earnings, she was eligible to receive a portion of her MFIP grant and child care assistance for her 6-year-old son.

Because Betty only works part-time, her job counsellor required her to spend 10 additional hours per week looking for full-time work or a second part-time job. Betty requested full time hours at the grocery store but her supervisor told her that he cannot give her more hours because her MFIP benefits would be jeopardized. Although this information is incorrect Betty remained convinced that she could not increase her hours at the store.

Betty agreed to spend 10 hours per week looking for additional work, but the demands of her job and the needs of her children made it difficult for her to meet this requirement. Betty struggles to fill out the job search calendars and other MFIP paperwork with her limited reading ability. Her MFIP grant was sanctioned when she failed to turn in a monthly job search calendar. The sanction reduced her grant and made Betty ineligible for child care assistance. Betty told the job counsellor it would be easier to look for a job on her own than to comply with the job counsellor's expectations. When Betty realized how little she would receive in assistance once the 30 per cent sanction took effect, she declined to return the forms verifying her rent amount. Betty was removed from MFIP assistance altogether, which also terminated health care coverage for her and her children.

currently widening between them and their employed sisters: 'While women's employment has been increasing, the employment rate of lone mothers has fallen since 1979 – from 48 per cent to 40 per cent by 1994. At the same time the proportion of married mothers in employment has risen from 53 per cent to 65 per cent.'[21] Therefore, added to our question of how we define work raised in the previous section in relation to parenting, and in particular the work of young child care and lone parents, is now the reality of the labour market, especially gender issues and discrimination. The statistic that 49 per cent of UK parents not working outside the home had no qualifications is stunning; this barrier is even more substantial when factors related to gender, race, marriage and age are considered.

Case studies detailed in Handler's research, *We the poor people,* suggest that this pattern of few qualifications amongst welfare

---

FIGURE 3.4: **Minnesota Case Studies: Nils Dybvig**   1998 US

Examples of budgets for welfare recipients in a 'generous' state

Anne:

Under MFIP, Anne's family of three received a total of $763 per month in assistance. Of that amount $532 is cash, and $231 is the food portion, which can only be redeemed for food. When she started working twenty hours per week at $4 per hour, she received monthly wages of $688. At this point the county started subtracting a portion of these wages from her grant, leaving her with $399 of assistance per month ($168. of cash and the entire $231 food portion). When combined with her wages her monthly income is $1087 leaving her considerably better off.

When she increased her hours to full-time her earnings increased to $1376 per month. At this point she became ineligible for further MFIP assistance. She will continue to receive medical benefits and child care assistance, although she will have to pay $22 per month towards her child care at her level of earnings.

Monthly income

	Cash	Food	Total
Anne's grant before starting work:	$532	$231	$763
Wages from work (20 hours x $8.00 per hour)	$688		
New Grant	$168	$231	
Total of grant + wages	$856	$231	$1087
Wages from work (40 x $8.00 per hour)	$1367		

Betty:

Betty's family of six received $1165 per month in MFIP assistance ($773 in cash and $392 in the food portion).

Betty started working twenty hours per week at $6.50 per hour, for monthly earnings of $563. Her MFIP assistance of $922 ($430 cash plus $392 in food) when added to her earnings gave her a total monthly income of $1485.

The first sanction reduced the cash portion of Betty's grant by $116. When the second sanction was going to take effect, Betty was notified that the state would pay a maximum of $530 toward her rent, even though her four-bedroom apartment costs $600 per month. After the $530 was paid, she would only receive $43 of food assistance. If she used $70 from her earnings to pay the remainder of her rent, she would have been left with $493 of her earnings and $43 in food assistance for the month. Instead, because Betty was removed from assistance for failing to fill out the required paperwork, her rent is unpaid and she is left with only her earnings of $563 which are insufficient to pay even her rent.

Monthly income

	Cash	Food	Total
Betty's grant before starting work:	$773	$392	$1165
Wages from work (20x$6.50 per hour)	$563		
New grant	$530	$392	
Total of grant + wages	$1093	$392	$1485
Total of grant + wages after first sanction	$977	$392	$1369
Total of grant + wages after second sanction	$563	$43	$606
(an additional would be $530 paid toward rent)			
Income without MFIP	$563		

applicants is similar in the US.[22] To illustrate these common themes, the case studies in figures 3.3 and 3.4 are supplied by a US employment counsellor, Nils Dybvig, and provide specific information for two families in the Midwest.

These contrasting case studies demonstrate both the opportunities that welfare 'reform' may offer and the oppressions. For Anne, a young mother with a work record and some qualifications, re-entering the formal work market external to the home can be an exhilarating experience, especially when well supported. The supports in this instance include the attention of the job counsellor, the opportunity to refresh work skills and an employer who provided career advancement at an early stage. The public, private and educational sectors all worked collaboratively. In the second situation, Betty is returning to work after a long absence from the formal work environment, has no clear work record or market-valued skills, and is ambivalent about the re-entry process. It is possible that her age, lack of skills and experience contributed to low self-esteem. There is no reference to being 'thrilled' or other energised feelings and optimism. Also, the employer undermines her re-entry by refusing, for questionable reasons, to extend her work hours and the administrative process overwhelms the recipient. In this instance, the administrative process, the lack of work experience, the public and employing environment, all combine to defeat this older applicant and keep her and her children poor. It is clear that the new system can work when positive factors such as qualifications, age, self-esteem, family-friendly employer all come into play. However, when there are negative factors, such as illiteracy, lack of employment record, low self-esteem, awkward employer, the system becomes fragile and quickly produces failure which is easily ascribed to the recipient rather than the system.

It is also breath-taking to visualize the impact of sanctions on already constrained budgets. In her presentation to the Minnesota Social Workers' Conference in 1999, a lone parent, Tammy, gave her budget to the audience and said, 'At the end of the month, however hard I work at it, my child goes without food. Every dollar counts.' The detailed budgets of the two recipients Anne and Betty confirm this reality.

It is evident that, without qualifications and employer encouragement to move from part-time to full-time work, the transition from 'welfare' to work outside the home, is a hard one. The numbers of persons to be supported makes a difference as well. Also, as illustrated in the direct debit to Betty of the costs of her four-bedroom apartment, the lack of affordable housing combined with rent vouchers sends already limited dollars to landlords instead of parents. This process puts children in jeopardy too.

A key step forward is to increase the match between skills, readiness and successful employment (meaning livable wage and benefits with career advancement opportunities and secure tenure of position). This match can be accomplished by encouraging private corporate initiatives to support people re-entering the workforce. For some states in the US there is increased creativity in terms of collaborations between the public and private sectors. For example the Xerox Business Services Corporation (XBS) is accepting trainees through the welfare-to-work programmes and combining both 'soft' and 'hard' orientation and training. The term 'soft' in this context, refers to preparation for work skills such as time management, presentation skills, communication, networking and social skills. The 'hard' training is job specific and tied into the notion of starting on a career ladder.

These corporate partnerships between the private sector and people in transition offer the best hope for people returning to work. However, without educational qualifications, the current minimum wage cannot lift families with children from poverty. Herbert, in his article, *Nike needs to raise workers' minimum wage, not minimum age*, reports that:

> The biggest problem with Nike is that its overseas workers make wretched, below subsistence wages…most of the workers in Nike factories in China and Vietnam make less than $2 a day, well below the subsistence levels in those countries…human rights organizations have been saying that overseas workers need to make at least $3 a day to cover basic good, shelter…Nike hasn't been listening…'[23]

This scenario is repeated for many corporations, including Cargill, Van Heusen and Gap and provides a back door to cheaper labour, which avoids raising the domestic standards of below minimum wages.

WHAT EDUCATION OPPORTUNITIES ARE PROVIDED IN THE CURRENT US POLICY

Perhaps the most crucial factor in these US case studies is the age of the unemployed parent. Statistics tell us that this is a common factor across countries – age at both ends of the spectrum – when childbearing in teenage years prevents gathering of qualifications and when being older than 40 and lacking an employment history locks people out of jobs. The UK Focus Files report that the UK and Australia 'have a higher proportion of lone parents under the age of 25 (14 per cent) than any other industrialized country' including the US which has 12 per cent.[24] One weekend in late summer 1998, in St Paul, Minnesota, a lonely immigrant woman killed her six children and attempted suicide; she was 24 years old and had her first child when she was 13.[25] The formal statistics may not touch us, but the desperation of struggling to bring up children in poverty, with no qualifications, as a teenager is a daily reality for too many of our families with children.

The stress for teenage and middle-aged recipients suggests the need for even wider layers of welfare reform including improved higher and further education support systems for adults and school education programmes for family planning. For example, why have Sweden, France and Italy been so successful in keeping teenage births low? What can the UK, US and Australia learn from Scandinavian education programmes which even in the 1980s in Sweden were explained as a top priority along with driving licences and the highway code: 'Teenagers in Sweden would no more have intercourse without contraception than run a stop light' is not a phrase which would be accurate in the US or the UK.[26] The *Time* research reports that young people at Project Hope in Chicago have little hope or sense of the future:'For young girls trapped in poverty, life offers few opportunities apart from getting pregnant. High school may seem pointless, even graduation is little guarantee of a job.' Bishop Earl Paul of Atlanta experiences a similar scenario: 'Pregnancy becomes one of the few accessible means of fulfilment. Nobody gets more attention than a girl who is pregnant.'

The UK Focus File statistic that '49 per cent of non-working lone parents in 1994 in the UK had no qualification' combined with the lack of life and work experience of teenage and young lone parents, clearly indicates the need for education and training of people in poverty. However, even though the school drop-out rate and lack of qualifications are equally problems for US income maintenance recipients, scant attention was paid to funding for education and training in the welfare reform legislation.

Hoffinger, of the US Results hunger lobby, writes: 'The euphoria caused by a booming economy, which now employs more people than ever before, does not take into account the growing phenomenon of the working poor in our country. A large number of the new jobs are at the lower end of the economic scale… A recent study conducted by Second Harvest, the largest chain of food banks in the country showed an increasing use of food shelves by working poor families with one or both parents employed, and by single parents, particularly women, with numbers of children. If welfare is to become work, we need to re-establish support for job-training (and education) which allows people to grow into good paying jobs which are needed in our economy…'[27] The Personal Responsibility and Work Opportunity Reconciliation Act P.L. 104–193 does not include job skills training, basic education or post secondary education. These needs are left to the discretion of individual states and the vision of private corporations and partnerships with human service. Certainly, the Minnesota Partnerships programme has listed a number of corporations, including Xerox, which have devised new orientation and support programs in order to connect people in transition back to the workplace.[28]

It is ironic to read the syndicated press report in September 1998 that the 'Road out of welfare shifts from education to work.' In a shift that is being felt by technical institutes and colleges, time and aid are being withdrawn:

> Five years ago, about 9,000 welfare recipients in Minnesota flocked to technical schools and colleges across the state, hoping to earn two-year degrees and to blossom under women's support groups, self-esteem classes and other TLC [tender loving care] from school staff members. By last year their numbers had dropped to 6,500. And only 3,900 were in school in July [1998]. Meanwhile, the feel-good programs are becoming history...Faced with fewer and shorter education options, students on welfare are following different tracks...some have dropped out of the welfare system and taken out students loans...others already enrolled, dropped out of the program at the urging of job counsellors...[29]

The funding had been available for education under the experimental and temporary Minnesota Family Investment Plan; now that this plan has been modified to comply with federal TANF rules, the education dollars have ceased because the politicians are committed to no tax increases for welfare and to the emphatic message – 'work is the solution'. While some welfare recipients may benefit from shorter term courses and strong partnerships with business, others will end up sooner in employment, but the quality, pay levels and opportunities for advancement are questionable. The questions are pressing now; they will be unavoidable by 2002. Some students have responded to the lack of support for higher education for welfare recipients by organizing themselves. Others give up and re-enter low paid work. This is demonstrated in states such as Connecticut where employers are offered a one-time grant for receiving people in transition from welfare with no guarantee of job security and Georgia where the WorkFirst programme results over the first 15 months reveal a high proportion of former welfare recipients returning to work. Parents formerly on welfare but now working may be counted as indicators of initial 'success' in the limited language of welfare reform. However, the downside for children is the stark statistic that only 14.2 per cent of parents tracked in Georgia, for example, are earning above minimum wage.[30]

In addition to factors related to characteristics of the recipient such as age, education, marital status, our analysis must add factors relating to the immediate environment of the recipient, such as the technical and college courses available, the nature of the state programme, the community service and family support network, the approach of the job counsellor, and the widest structural issues of employment policy, public/private partnerships and family-friendly employers.

FIGURE 3.5: **Midland Bank UK**

A family-friendly employer[31]

The Midland Bank employs a higher percentage of women than men, although senior positions continue to be occupied by men. Since the 1980s the Bank has been an innovator in providing family benefits. One key reason for this initiative was the cost to the Bank of replacing experienced employees who left their positions after childbirth.

Characteristics of the Bank's approach

1 Staff position: Equal Opportunities Manager.
2 Since 1988 a nursery programme, with over 100 nurseries established by 1996, open to all primary carers among employees (both part and full-time).
3 A career break for carers, initially intended for infant care, extended in 1995 to all caring situations. The career break is for up to five years, an employee can re-apply on a 'fast track' to regain their position or a related position.
4 All women in the UK are entitled by law to 14 weeks maternity leave (regardless of time in position). The Midland has extended this to 46 weeks for its employees: 11 before birth and 35 after.
5 Paternity leave was introduced in January 1996.
6 Family leave = 5 days paid leave per year for sick children.
7 Flexible working hours: including benefits for part-time workers and negotiable work periods.

THE PROSPECTS FOR CHILDREN WHEN WORK COMES FIRST: FAMILY-FRIENDLY EMPLOYERS AND CHILDCARE

While the concept of the 'family-friendly' employer is still gaining currency in both the US and the UK, a vivid illustration of how feasible and helpful to children (in supportive arrangements for sick leave, maternity leave, child care and sustained employment through family change and crisis) it can be is the Midland Bank in Britain.

In the US, individual states vary widely in their expectation of employers to collaborate in tackling poverty. The Midland Bank offers an example for many countries, in its attention to market trends, increasing numbers of women with children entering the workforce and 'the impact on the bottom line profits.' Research in the 1980s revealed that too many women employees were being lost to maternity leave, and the Institute of Management Studies showed that 'the replacement costs of an experienced employee were roughly equal to his/her annual employment costs; it was calculated that it was costing the bank around 15 million pounds a year to lose such a high percentage of women.' Clearly the policy decisions made sound business sense; they have also led to a reputation for the Midland Bank that it is an organization with vision and the flexibility within management to respond to demographic changes and the call for more family-friendly work environments.[32] This last example of a family-supportive workplace is cause for optimism concerning the way re-entry to employment outside the home can be established. However, it is not yet the norm in the US. Furthermore, a question lingers: is this 'friendliness' reserved for the middle class? As noted earlier, the poor are viewed negatively for desiring the same options.

A central element in the family-friendly employer lexicon is adequate funding for child care. For the US there is a highly uneven pattern of public and private child care provision. In statistics entitled *Federal and Related State Child Care Funding for Low-Income Families*, it is evident that geographical differences are very significant in terms of resources available to families with children.[33] The Minnesota programmes have been quoted widely in this book as 'generous' as compared with many other states and these statistics confirm that Minnesota is in the ranking of 30 states that plan, submit and draw down 100 per cent of the federal financing available. Two states, Louisiana and Mississippi, draw down less than five per cent of dollars available and these states have the highest rates of poverty amongst Black children. However, even in the more 'generous' states, there has been a struggle to maintain adequate child care facilities in the public sector. Senator Pat Piper for Minnesota lays out the problems:

> When the state Legislature returned to develop the 1998 Supplemental Budget, facts show the need for child care was greater than had been anticipated and in the winter of 1998 the waiting list had grown to 3,300 working families…the senate earmarked $10 million for child care intending to eliminate two thirds of the waiting list…in

negotiations with the House this was reduced by half. Our State allocates $7 billion biennially for the thirteen years of educational opportunities for those in the k-12 system. Why aren't we ready yet to commit the appropriate dollars for our state's littlest children...[34]

Thus child care provisions from state to state are very uneven and rarely adequately funded even in states which support public expenditure on children; the existence of family-friendly employers is minimal, and in the atmosphere of WorkFirst, the current prospects for children experiencing poverty are bleak.

The Children's Defense Fund informs us that one in two children of colour in the US are in poverty. While social workers see the consequences of neglecting children daily in the cost of foster care and residential settings, while probation officers pick up the pieces in the correctional setting, the opportunities for prevention are clear:

FIGURE 3.6: **Problems of poor and non poor children**   1993 US

	poor	non poor
Infant deaths per 1,000	13.5%	8.5%
Percentage of live births	13%	7.3%
Low birth weight	10.2%	5.5%
Inadequate prenatal care	43.1%	15.6%
% of students repeating a grade K3-12	31.3%	15.4%

(seecopy of the figures quoted by the Children's Defense Fund from Federman, M. et al. What does it mean to be poor in America? *Monthly Labor Review*, 119.3–17. 15)

In drafting UK welfare reform legislation the 1998 drive of the Children's Defense Fund, 'Leave no child behind,' could well help focus public attention on the ways to prevent the waste of talent and possibility represented in the consequences of child poverty.

While we wait for the focus of attention to turn toward children, human service agencies continue to receive more child abuse and neglect reports than they can manage.[35] It may be that a long-term effect for some mothers who manage to get on a career ladder will be an improvement in circumstances for their children, but there is a strong tide of child poverty to turn, complicated by racism and lack of equitable access to services. *The Statistical Record of Children*[36] confirms the increases in rates of poverty for children from the 1980s to the 1990s:

The (US) child poverty rate increased 17 per cent during the 1980s. The rate increased in 37 states. While all children were affected, the increase was greatest for Hispanic children, whose poverty rate grew by 25 per cent over the decade.[37] These rates of poverty for children have continued into the millennium and are compounded by lack of health coverage and strong disparity concerning access to health, nutrition and education according to race, see figure 3.7.

FIGURE 3.7: **Statistical record of children**   1994 US

- About 12 million American children suffer from chronic hunger.
- The problem is worst in some Southern states, where more than one-fourth of all children regularly go hungry.
- The hunger rate is more than 18 per cent in New York, South Dakota and California.
- Initiation of Prenatal Care according to race of mother (1985):
  All mothers: 76.2%
  White mothers: 79.2%
  Black mothers: 61.5%
  Hispanic mothers: 61.2%

Structural issues of access to medical coverage, employment and income constantly lead to disparities according to race with white mothers and children faring better than Black families. Cornell West calls for policy makers' attention regarding these disparities in access to the means for basic family well-being:

> We must accent the best of each other even as we point out the vicious effects of our racial divide and the pernicious consequences of our maldistribution of wealth and power. We simply cannot enter the twenty-first century at each other's throats, even as we acknowledge the weighty forces of racism, patriarchy, economic inequality, homophobia, and ecological abuse on our necks...None of us alone can save the nation or world. But each of us can make a positive difference if we commit ourselves to do so.[38]

The recent US welfare reform emphasizes returning to work as the solution to child and family health, education, housing and nutritional needs. However, all children go through the transitions and challenges of childhood that demand the attention of parents and extended family. The current emphasis on working at all costs means that lone, mainly female, parents are caught in traps of not taking time off to care for minor symptoms even though that may lead to children become more seriously sick. It is suggested, in the Statistical Record of Children, that families experiencing poverty have children hospitalized for longer periods and that this may be connected to the lack of preventive services available to them, or the lack of time to take them up and the consequent worsening of the child's situation. Furthermore, the younger the infant is when exposed to group (child care centre or baby-minding) germs, the more vulnerable to succumbing to infection. This suggests a self-defeating policy where mothers of infants are encouraged to return to work within a six-week period in the US and then have difficulty establishing a strong attendance record. Maternity and paternity leave is amongst the shortest in the world in the US, compared to much longer periods in Europe.

In times of economic depression, for example in the 1930s, the US responded with work creation programs and education initiatives. What government intervention in terms of educational opportunities and work creation is currently available? Hage describes the contrasting situations from state to state:

> Oregon will fix up an applicant with social workers and job counsellors, while Wisconsin won't even consider a welfare application until the client has been job hunting for 30 days. New York State is pouring money into public-sector community service jobs, while California is betting on the private sector. Tennessee cuts off your benefits after 18 months as a motivational tool, while 27 states will keep sending you a check for five years (until 2002)...[39]

Children, all 14 million plus of them in poverty in the US, take the brunt of lack of education services, sanctions for unsuccessful job search, family 'unfriendly' employers and lack of child care.

CONCLUSIONS AND CHAPTER SUMMARY

Essentially, it has been clear for centuries that the social welfare and economic vitality of a nation are intertwined, and while the individual characteristics of people are important in their response to opportunity, far more crucial from a policy maker's point of view are the structural arrangements that either support or destroy local initiatives.

It is with some irony that we trace the economic upheavals of Europe in past centuries and see that when the wealthy turn their back on the poor, it is often with desperate results. Marie Antoinette is the most visited symbol: responding to news that people were rebelling because they had no bread, her retort 'then let them eat cake' seems absurdly removed from reality. With the French and later Russian Revolutions there were immediate responses in British policies for people experiencing poverty. Similarly, following the First and Second World wars we see a spate of policies to improve the conditions of the poor, from the 'Homes Fit for Heroes' of the 1920s to the full scale 'Welfare State' of the Beveridge plan in the 1940s. For the relatively young republic of the US, the pioneer, 'go it alone', independent spirit myths of the nineteenth century have been allowed to continue despite the economic and social complexity of the twenty-first century which makes the 'independent' life impossible for any of us. If we recognize the tight connection between the number of welfare recipients and the buoyancy of the economy, then we recognize that structural rather than personal factors determine rates of poverty amongst families and children. If we move from blaming the so called 'dependent individual' to scrutinizing the structure of our educational, social and employment worlds, we are more likely to find the keys to attacking poverty. However, the shift needs a simultaneous sea change in political rhetoric and public understanding.

Currently the picture of 'back to work' policy is very mixed. Evaluation research in Wisconsin, Oregon or Georgia which identifies success as reduction of the number of people receiving welfare will continue to find such 'success'. However, the continued poverty of children, uneven childcare and distressed lone parents is the reality for too many families where 'back to work' means below minimum wage and job insecurity. A crisis hovers in communities such as Philadelphia where cut-off dates are bringing families with children closer to destitution (see Appendix 1 for the text of Mayor Rendell's speech, March 7th, 1999).

Several unintended consequences of welfare reform are becoming apparent. These include:

- confusion concerning the reasons for sanctions which means that parents are left feeling that the rules are intimidating, resulting in lack of take-up of Medicaid, childcare funding and food stamps;
- a misfiring of the legislators' intent concerning 'sanctions' intended

as incentive and in practice experienced as the arbitrary and oppressive action of administrators;
- an increase in the numbers of children admitted to foster care; and
- uneven childcare provision and increased use of 'informal' arrangements which put children at risk.[40]

Much heed was paid to the Manpower Demonstration Research Corporation (MDRC) study which showed that short term 'labour force attachment' supports, such as counselling, job preparation and training were more effective in reducing the 'welfare rolls' than longer term investment in higher education.[41] Yet analysis of the impact on children when their parents take a job at any price shows the continuation of their poverty under new status – they become the 'workpoor'. This is not to say that welfare reform is without positive effect in terms of increasing public awareness of the effects of poverty on children, developing the potential for public–private partnership and expanding 'family friendly' employment. However, no 'success' can be claimed in terms of reducing the poverty of children until the following issues are adequately addressed:

- the inclusion of people employed in caring for children under three in the home as 'workers';
- educational provision in the legislation to increase the qualifications of people receiving welfare to enhance their employment prospects;
- recognition that moving from welfare to lowest paid employment does not mean longer term improvements in standards of living (indeed it means that families continue to be acutely vulnerable, especially in times of economic down turn);
- the need for an increase in licensed child care to meet demand; and
- recognition that children do best when they receive adequate nutrition, clothing, housing and live in an anguish-free home environment.

The cost of maintaining children outside the home in foster care or residential settings is high in contrast to the lower per capita cost of income maintenance to families experiencing poverty. It is ironic to read of the increase in demand for 'crisis nurseries' and homeless shelters and to witness the reality of the assessment that 'the 1996 federal welfare reform law may increase the need for child welfare services and drive up the costs of child protection' at the very time the emphasis is on cutting costs.[42] Work first, pay later, is becoming the reality for a society that rejects the idea of collective freedom from want, particularly for its youngest children.

The typology of resilient families developed by writers such as McCubbin and Saleeby perhaps speaks more vividly to the objectives we should have for welfare policy reform in the millennium: resilient families have extended community supports and child care arrangements, they have adequate finances for basic provisions, they have coping skills, work opportunity, time for their children, sense of future, sense of humour and influence over their lives.[43] The opportunities and positive aspects of US welfare reform are represented by recipients such as Anne (see case study p53), who has gained new energy from her successful job search and feels encouraged by her job counsellor and employer. Her situation demonstrates the combination of factors that can spell 'success' and resilience in maintaining income: public-private partnerships; corporate involvement; networking for isolated mothers, and raised public awareness of the repercussions for children unless they can be lifted out of poverty. However, for people with more than one child, who are over thirty-five, who lack qualifications and employment history and have few work-readiness skills, the current policy is seriously inadequate, particularly in the way it makes children even more vulnerable to poverty than before and liable to destitution in 2002 and beyond.

NOTES

1 Minnesota Department of Human Services, Statewide Minnesota Family Investment Program. DHS, 1997.

2 Editorial, *Star Tribune*, Minneapolis, 3 February 2000.

3 R Simpson & R Walker, *Europe: for richer or poorer?*, CPAG, 1993.

4 L Engelhardt, *Bread for the World*, BFTW, 1996.

5 Simpson & Walker, (note 3).

6 C Germain, *Human Behavior in the Social Environment*, Columbia, 1994.

7 National Commission on Children, *Beyond Rhetoric*, US 46, 1996.

8 T Bowman, Summary of parent focus groups, Minneapolis: Southside Family Nurturing Center, 1999.

9 J Berryman, *Unemployment and Depression*, University of Leicester, 1986.

10 A Kotlowitz, *There are no children here*, Doubleday, 1993.

11 P Peterson, Get the rich off the dole, *Time*, 31 October 1988.

12 M Wright Edelman, *Families in Peril*, Children's Defense Fund, 1997.

13 *Poverty Matters*, Children's Defense Fund, 1999.

14 M Federman et al, 'What does it mean to be poor in America?', *Monthly Labor Review*, pp119–3–17, 1998.

15 W Hutton, *The Observer*, 2 August 1998.

16 O Gill, *Parenting Under Pressure*, Barnardo's, 1992.

17 S K Long & S J Clark, *The New Child Care Block Grant: State Funding Choices and their Implications*, The Urban Institute, Series A, no. A-12, October 1997, The Urban Institute, 1997.

18 L Rainwater, *Youth Services Review 17*, 1995, pp11–41.

19 J Handler, *The Poverty of Welfare Reform*, Yale, 1997.

20 Welfare Reform Focus Files, (note 20).

21 Welfare Reform Focus Files, (note 20).

22 J Handler, *We the Poor People*, 1995.

23 B Herbert, 'Nike Needs to Raise Worker's Minimum Wage, not Minimum Age', *New York Times*, 26 May 1998.

24 Welfare Reform Focus Files, (note 20).

25 *Star Tribune*, 6 September 1998.

26 *Time*, 'Children having Children', 9 December 1985.

27 P Hoffinger, *To get people off welfare, train them*, Results hunger lobby groups, Minneapolis, 1998.

28 *22 Partnerships Get Down to Business*, McKnight Report, 1998.

29 J Hopfensperger, *Star Tribune*, 28 September 1998.

30 Georgia WorkFirst Program Results: ww2.state.ga.us/BROC/peach.html.

31 S Lewis & J Lewis, eds., *Work-Family Challenge Rethinking Employment*, Sage, 1996.

32 Since reporting this study, the Midland Bank have been taken over and the maintenance of these policies has yet to be seen. Their practice and intent remain, however, an example to other employers.

33 From the US House of Representatives, Committee on Ways and Means, 1996, Green Book, Fiscal Year federal and state spending on Title IVA.

34 P Piper, *Star Tribune, Parents moving from welfare to work desperately need child care*, 15 May 1998.

35 M Courtney, 'The Costs of Child Protection in the Context of Welfare Reform'. *The Future of Children: Protecting Children From Abuse and Neglect*, Vol 8, No. 1, Spring, 1998.

36 L Schmittroth, *The Statistical Record of Children*, Gale Research, 1994.

37 Schmittroth, (note 36).

38 C West, *Race Matters*, Vintage Books, 1994.

39 S Hage, A25 *Star Tribune*, 30 August 1998.

40 B Fuller & S Kagan, *Remember the Children: Mothers Balance Work and Child Care under Welfare Reform*, Graduate School of Education-PACE University of California, Berkeley 94720, 2000.

41 S Freedman, & D Friedlander, *The JOBS evaluation: Early findings on program impacts in three sites*, The Urban Institute, 1995.

42 Courtney, (note 35).

43 D Saleeby, *The Strengths Perspective in Social Work Practice*, 2nd Edition, Longman, 1998.

4 UK policy designed to combat child poverty

by Karen Lyons

Ideas about what we mean by 'welfare' are very different on either side of the Atlantic, notwithstanding the British adoption of the narrow definition of welfare, taken up by advocates of welfare rights. Additionally, the geographical position of the UK, facing North America on the one hand and Europe on the other, and its varied political history, through its links with former colonies (now Commonwealth countries), and, more recently, its membership of the European Union have contributed to different understandings and emphases in its approach to social welfare and development of policies.

Nevertheless, the influence of the US has periodically been significant; for instance, in the mid-1960s when, following the 'rediscovery of poverty', the UK drew on some of the ideas emerging from the US War on Poverty programme to inform its own initiatives (the Education Priority Areas and Community Development programmes), and more recently, through the adoption of language and policies in the 1980s and 1990s which have led up to the recent changes with which this book is concerned.

This chapter considers the circumstances in which 'reform of the welfare state' has been a central preoccupation, initially of the Conservative administrations (1979–97), and now of the 'New Labour' government. The chapter is mainly concerned with the changes that have recently been made or are imminent, and which might be seen to address a declared concern of the current government – child poverty. A statement by the Social Security Secretary, Alistair Darling, in 1999 re-committed the government to a target of abolishing child poverty within twenty years, coinciding with the maximum time scale proposed for evaluation of the success of its wider welfare reform programme. In ten years the government aims to halve the number of children in poverty, estimated at 4.5 million in 1997/8.[1]

Other estimates suggest that, of eleven million children in England and Wales, one in three live in poverty (Shinman, 1999) and the proportions are similar for Scotland and Northern Ireland.[2] With reference to income distribution in general, research has shown that, apart from some narrowing of the gap between rich and poor in the mid-1990s, the gap between the richest and poorest people in the UK increased significantly during the 1980s and by the late 1990s was greater than at any time since the late 1940s.[3]

A major plank of the government's plan to address welfare reform has been the welfare-to-work policy discussed below (with some reference to related concerns about the labour market and family-friendly employment policies). There has also been some recognition of the need for new initiatives in relation to childcare provision, 'family support' and community development programmes, and these are discussed in the penultimate section. There are other policy developments affecting low income families, for instance in the juvenile justice field, which demonstrate government intentions to emphasize the responsibility of parents for their children's behaviours as well as care, as in the Crime and Disorder Act 1998, and towards people with disabilities (who are included in the welfare-to-work approach) but these are beyond the scope of this chapter. The concluding section considers how far these policy changes have been subject to US influences relative to those of the European Union, and also assesses the likelihood that child and family poverty will be reduced by the welfare reform in train.

'REFORMING THE WELFARE'

A post-war consensus view of the 'benefits to all' of the Welfare State began to be challenged in the 1960s, prompted by rising levels of expenditure, particularly in the field of financial support (then called national assistance) and by findings from academic research that many children and families were still living in poverty. One outcome of these findings and of increasing dissatisfaction in other policy areas was the establishment of pressure groups to advocate for the needs of particular minority groups (such as CPAG in relation to child poverty).

After a generation of increasing expectations about 'provision by the state', from the cradle to the grave, there began a slow resurgence of the voluntary sector in the UK. New organizations (initially often small and local) were added to the few long-established charities and other agencies in the personal social services field which had continued to provide financial help or direct care to individuals whose particular needs were recognized as being inadequately met by the state. This shift might be seen as the beginning of the diversification of social welfare provisions which was to be accelerated and extended into the commercial sector and back into the family and community under the Conservatives, post-1979.

Developments in the infrastructure of the social welfare system also need to be seen against a backcloth of rising political consciousness and concern for economic and civil rights across a range of groups, partly influenced by developments in the US but also evident in other parts of Europe. The 1960s in the UK saw the beginning of feminist and subsequently anti-racist movements (and the resurgence of nationalist activities in Northern Ireland in the face of economic discrimination on denominational grounds), and later still, establishment of groups concerned with 'gay rights' and the rights of people with disabilities. Many of these activities were based on self-help (or, more properly, mutual help) and collective principles and, in theory, crossed the class divisions with which previous policy makers and sociological analysis had apparently been so concerned. They marked the onset of a period of dissent and 'interest group' politics.[4] The sense of dissatisfaction with social policies was compounded by the advent of the oil crisis in the mid-1970s resulting in significant economic problems and loss of faith in the political party of the day and the Welfare State itself.[5] The scene was set for a swing to the right in British voting habits and the onset in 1979 of the Thatcher era.

One of the stated intentions of Margaret Thatcher in the post-election period was to 'roll back the welfare state' and much of the rhetoric of the 1980s and early 1990s was concerned with the 'crisis in welfare' and the 'dismantling of the welfare state'. The policies of successive Conservative governments owed much to Thatcher's admiration of 'The American Way', and had a profound effect on the infrastructure of service delivery in all fields of social welfare and on the culture of organizations and society as a whole.[6] However, some aspects of the welfare state have perhaps proved more durable than might have been anticipated, leaving the way open for renewed efforts at 'welfare reform', but with some continuities, with the return to power of a 'New Labour' Government in 1997. These are discussed more fully after a brief consideration of some of the significant changes introduced in the 1980s and early 1990s.

Basic to Thatcherite policy change was the belief that market principles should apply in all sectors of the economy, including those previously regarded as being 'public sector' (including water and other utilities) or related aspects of social and health care and financial support. Neo-liberal principles (as espoused by Hayek) would ensure greater efficiency and economy through competition in service provision, and enable greater choice and the exercise of individual responsibility by 'consumers' of services. Individual responsibility included a return to greater reliance on the community or 'the family' (or parents) as reflected in the passing of the National Health Service and Community Care Act in 1990 and the Child Support Act in 1991. The first was to place more responsibility on family members or community provisions in respect of people (including some children with disabilities) who would previously have been cared for in hospitals, while the second more particularly attempted to shift financial support for children in lone parent families from the state to the absent parent. The latter change had a direct bearing on the circumstances of many children in low income families and will be discussed further later in this chapter.

The private (commercial for profit) sector was also to assume greater importance in all aspects of welfare, including the provision of insurance-based pension and health care schemes. While some developments in this area would be consistent with funding patterns in other EU countries, and even more so in the US, the need for some continuing state provision was to some extent revealed by the difficulty of some vulnerable groups in getting such insurance. This was highlighted in the case of people suffering from HIV AIDS, it was not until the advent of some scandals about the mis-selling of pension schemes to elderly victims that financial regulation and some rethinking about pension provision came onto the political agenda, largely under the new Labour government.

Similarly, comparatively high levels of home ownership in the UK were to be enhanced by selling off local authority housing stock to people who already had tenancies, and the needs of (a minority of) people for subsidized accommodation were to be met through differently financed and organized Housing Associations. T̶ ̶ ̶ ̶ ̶ ̶ ̶ ̶ ̶ ̶ supported the Conservative vision of a 'home-owning dem̶ again could be seen to be flawed when an economic down end of the 1980s resulted in a steep rise in unemployment number of properties being repossessed. Apart from the psychological stress caused to families, there were real problems about the re-housing of such adults and children since the local authority housing stock had been significantly reduced (often to the least desirable properties or estates where average incomes were so low that tenants had been unable to afford to buy in the first instance) and Housing Association provision was in high demand and catered for the needs of particular groups.

One of the main aims of various policy changes in the financial support field in the 1980s (and into the 1990s) was the reduction of public expenditure but, increasingly, also to reduce 'welfare dependency' – an idea directly influenced by US thinking, as discussed in earlier chapters. A decrease in the number of people in receipt of financial support has been achieved through a number of measures, many of which have directly impacted on families with children (though not necessarily young children). For instance, one of the early measures of the Thatcher government (culminating in a new Social Security Act in 1986) was an attempt to limit the range of grants available (and the degree of discretion in the operation of provisions) and included the stopping of 'special payments'. The latter were grants to people, often families, who needed to replace large items such as bedding or a cooker. Under alternative arrangements a cash-limited Social Fund was established through which loans could be made in some circumstances.

However, the low level of financial support provided made the repayment of such loans a near impossibility and sometimes resulted in low income families seeking high interest credit from loan sharks or seeking help from social workers.[7] This might take the form of applications for one-off grants to 'charities' or the payment of 'Section 1 money' from local authority Social Services Departments. Section 1 of the Children and Young Persons Act 1969 enabled social workers to make emergency payments to 'prevent the reception into care of children' and was not intended to substitute for or augment other means of financial support. While the ease or difficulty of securing such 'payments' partly depended on where families lived, this avenue to additional support was limited, but not done away with, when new legislation superseded the CYPA 1969. Under the 1989 Children Act, Section 17, assistance (including cash payments) may be made 'in exceptional circumstances', 'subject to conditions, including repayment', although the degree of discretion exercised in this field, as in others, was also curtailed, not least through the rise of 'managerialism'.[8]

There are two main reasons why child poverty continues to exist. The first relates to unemployment of the main breadwinner (or in some cases to people being in insecure and low wage jobs) and the second relates to change in the structure of families and the increase in lone parent households. More than 1 million children live in two-parent families where there is no wage-earner, but more than half the children in poverty live in lone parent families.[9] Both groups have been the focus of policy change as part of the wider agenda of reforming the welfare state, and are considered in turn.

UNEMPLOYMENT

Unemployment levels and the costs of unemployment to the tax payer (since only about 20 per cent of unemployed people in the UK receive insurance-based benefits) were a constant source of concern to the Conservative government and various measures were made to 'contain the problem'. These included changes to the benefits system which over time both reduced the value to claimants of unemployment benefits and reduced the numbers of people eligible for unemployment benefit and other forms of financial support. In relation to the first it has been suggested that the ratio of benefits to paid employment fell from 79 per cent (in 1978) to 60 per cent in 1983/4 and that in that year, 20 per cent of 'dole' claimants received an income from benefits worth only half of their previous earnings.[10]

In relation to the second, one such measure was the removal of income support from young people over school leaving age (16 years) but under the age of majority (18 years). It was assumed that such young people should live with and be supported by their families, and if they remained in school, payment of child benefit (see later) would be continued. If young people chose to leave home they should seek employment, although the realities of the labour market meant that special provisions had to be made for this group, which centred on short-term training programmes. These were aimed at increasing the young person's 'employability' but since some areas lacked jobs (particularly for relatively unskilled and inexperienced workers) the scheme was criticized as offering only short-term 'solutions' with no real prospect of subsequent work. There was also a significant rise in youth homelessness which in part was attributed to the strains caused within families supporting unemployed teenagers.

More generally, the introduction in 1996 of a 'Jobseeker's Allowance' (in place of income support and unemployment benefit for unemployed adults) marked the formal beginnings of the welfare-to-work policy. The new terminology directly reflected the language, and began to emulate the policies, of the US in this field, and would be further developed under New Labour, as discussed in the middle of this chapter.

INCREASE IN LONE PARENTS

The other major cause of child poverty over the past few decades has been the increase in the number of lone parent families, usually headed by women, many of whom receive income support from the state. The proportion of children living with only their mothers rose from around 6 per cent in 1972 to 18 per cent in 1996/7, with a further 1 per cent living with only a father, totalling 2.7m children. In 1995, 41 per cent of these households had an average weekly income of £100 or less, while only 10 per cent had a weekly income of £350 or more (compared with 65 per cent of 'couple families'). Studies by the Institute for Fiscal Studies have suggested that 75 per cent of children in lone parent families live in poverty compared with only 18 per cent in two-parent households.[11]

Apart from the significant likelihood of having a low income family, lone parents have also periodically been subject to public hostility and stigma, which 'welfare reform' has sometimes fuelled rather than mitigated. The 1980s and early 1990s saw a 'moral crusade' against the rise in the numbers of lone parents, mainly mothers, and the associated decline of 'the family', by which was meant the two-parent (preferably married), nuclear family. Lone parents have sometimes been typified as young, unmarried women who have allegedly become pregnant deliberately, in order to secure local authority housing. The fact that 'teenage mothers' constitute a relatively small proportion of all lone parents has tended to be disregarded, as have the particular needs of this group. Overall, in the 1990s lone parent households constituted only 7 per cent of all households in Britain, and of these the largest group (4 per cent) were divorced parents with children, while never-married parents comprised 2 per cent and the remaining 1 per cent were widows/widowers.[12] Thus, the facts tend to contradict the reality of a situation which has been subject to negative press coverage, although recent reports suggest that 'teenage pregnancies' constitute the fastest growing group within lone parent families, and they are currently the subject of renewed attention (see later).

One aspect of policy change aimed at reducing child poverty – but also, and perhaps more significantly, at discouraging lone parenthood and shifting responsibility for income support from the state (back) to parents – was the passing of the Child Support Act in 1991, brought into operation through the establishment of the Child Support Agency in 1993. This agency was charged with identifying the name and whereabouts of the absent parent (usually father) and ensuring the payment of maintenance for the relevant child/children, in some cases through 'attachment of earnings'.

The Agency was criticized in the early stages of operation for disregarding settlements already reached through the courts (usually in the case of marital breakdown). In fact, the whole basis of this Act can be seen as shifting responsibility from the Courts and legal system to a bureaucratic system intended to contain rising costs in this area. It has been speculated that this was another manifestation of the curbing of professional powers and discretion, which, in this case might have been seen as colluding with parents in negotiating 'clean break settlements'. These released one parent (usually the father) from further financial and other responsibilities while leaving the way open for the parent caring for children to claim benefits from the state. Decision making was thus transferred to bureaucrats (or managers) bound by technical formulas with regard to assessment of benefits or conditions.

Another of the early criticisms was the inflexible, inappropriate and in some cases unworkable nature of the formulas devised to assess the payments which absent fathers would be required to make and the resulting hardship sometimes caused to children of new relationships. Other criticisms include the inefficiency of the agency (slow assessments and inaccurate payments) and the requirement placed on women to name the father. In relation to the last, it is possible for women to decline to name the father in specific circumstances, usually if they have left a relationship because of violence.

Fathers also complained about the requirement to meet financial costs when this does not necessarily assist their access to children. Indeed, unmarried fathers have financial responsibilities but no parental rights. Unintended consequences were also apparent when the calculations of amounts to be paid disregarded the costs of step-families and shifted poverty from children in one family to those in another.[13] Various amendments have periodically been made to the staffing and regulation, and at the time of writing, the workings of this Act and of the agency itself are under review again. Policy development in this area can be seen to replicate developments in the US but there are also similar schemes in operation in many other European countries (for instance, in Germany), and this seems to be an area where policy change had chimed with some sections of public opinion, notwithstanding criticisms.

The issue of lone parent families also intersects with continuing debate about the expectations that lone mothers should be self-supporting. Lister has suggested that the Conservative government did not in fact take Britain down the road of most other OECD countries in requiring lone mothers to work, but it did begin to shift expectations and attitudes in this direction through the CSA and some of the social security changes of the 1980s and 1990s.[14] Recent policy developments under New Labour in relation to lone parent families are examined in the wider context of welfare-to-work policies.

Before proceeding to examine more recent policy changes under the general welfare-to-work heading, it should be noted in passing that another issue highlighted under the Conservative administrations but continuing to receive attention under New Labour concerns fraudulent claims for various kinds of financial support, including benefits related to ill health or invalidity and unemployment (eg. where, in fact, the person has undeclared earnings). Fraud is also claimed to be rife in the area of housing benefits. Concern about fraud has undoubtedly exacerbated negative attitudes among officials and the wider public, in which 'claimants' of various kinds feel stigmatized as well as poor.

Finally, notwithstanding Conservative assertions of 'family values' in relation to some of their policy changes, the New Labour government came to power in 1997 on a wave of disillusionment with politicians, not least because of the evident hypocrisy of some whose personal relationships and public dealings were the subject of 'scandals' fully reported in the media. It might also be assumed that there were concerns by some about the rate and direction of policy change in a host of areas, including the social welfare sector, and that there were expectations that, while some changes might not be reversed, their effects might be mitigated under a political party which had traditionally espoused a different philosophy and values.

However, an early initiative of the new government was the production of a Green Paper (1998) in which the rationale for the 'reform of welfare' was made clear. One of the problems included an eight-fold increase in social security expenditure in real terms over fifty years of the welfare state's existence: social security had risen proportionately from 14 per cent of government expenditure in 1949 to 33 per cent in 1978.[15] Yet, despite concerns about welfare spending 'spiralling out of control,' fuelled in the media by 'scares' about the costs of particular groups of welfare claimants (for example, most recently, refugees and asylum seekers), it has been suggested elsewhere that expenditure was in fact fairly stable over the period 1982–96 and has actually declined as a proportion of GDP.

Deans suggests that successive governments have chosen to restrict welfare spending, or have increased it only when poor economic performance, as reflected in high unemployment, has increased the numbers of people entitled to benefits.[16] Similarly, while British welfare spending may seem generous relative to American assumptions and practices, Britain can be compared unfavourably on this criterion with other members of the European Union although other EU countries, as indicated earlier, generally find a greater part of their systems through insurance schemes rather than through taxation.

Other problems cited in the Green Paper include the following:

- although 73 per cent of all adults of working age were in work this figure dropped to only just over half in some major cities (Glasgow, Newcastle, Manchester, Liverpool and some London boroughs);
- on average, almost one in five working age households did not have a breadwinner (compared with less than one in ten in 1979);
- there were still significant differences in average gross weekly earnings between those holding degrees and those without qualifications, with the former earning nearly double the average salary of the latter, and the latter being significantly more likely to experience unemployment, and for longer;
- the proportion of women in the work force had increased from 59 per cent in 1973 to 67 per cent in 1995 (though details about the type of employment and pay levels were omitted); and
- the number of divorces in England and Wales had nearly doubled through the 1970s and 1980s, having already doubled in the 1960s, averaging 155,000 by 1995, such that one in four children had experienced family break-up, and one in five families are headed by a lone parent.

These and other statistics, including about pensions and about people with disabilities, constituted the basis for the government's concerns and intentions.

WELFARE-TO-WORK POLICIES

Notwithstanding a good majority in Parliament, there were a number of major challenges facing the new government in 1997, if it were to achieve a longer-term goal of gaining a second term in office. These included establishing trust among the commercial and industrial sector, maintaining a healthy economy, and not alienating a segment of new voters (attuned to a culture of individualism and enterprise and sometimes typified as 'Middle England') while 'keeping on board' traditional Labour Party supporters. In fact, the Government in its early stages declared its intention to stick to spending plans inherited from the Conservatives, and an increase in investment in public services such as health and education, which some voters had hoped for, initially failed to materialize.

However, the challenge of addressing the increased gap between the 'haves and have nots' was also recognized: proportionally more people were 'poor' – in receipt of less than half the national average income – in 1997 than in 1979. While the traditional labour movement had had an overt goal of promoting redistribution through its fiscal and social policies, the New Labour government announced a 'third way' of proceeding (including tackling issues of inequality and social injustice) which showed some continuities with measures promoted under the Conservatives. However, the new Government's intention to 'tackle social division and inequality' in society, was indicated in a speech by the Prime Minister in December 1997, when he announced the setting up of a new entity, the Social Exclusion Unit.

The Unit could be seen to be informed by policy developments in Europe, where the notion of marginalization and exclusion of groups of people in poverty and/or otherwise different from the 'mainstream population', had given rise to a number of initiatives and programmes from which Britain under the Conservatives had largely dissociated itself. The work of the three Task Forces initially set up under the Social Exclusion Unit involved a reconsideration of the forms and consequences of poverty and made some attempt to examine the problems of particular groups in ways which acknowledged the inter-relationships between different forms of disadvantage. It also reintroduced the notion of wider 'government consultation' about problems and possible policy directions – a practice that had been noticeably absent, or extremely selective, in the Thatcher years. This (and some of the subsequent mechanisms for developing new initiatives) can also be seen as a demonstration of the government's attempt to introduce 'joined up thinking' about problems and possible solutions, not bound by the conventional wisdom and territorial disputes of central government and local authority departments.

Alongside the work of the Social Exclusion Unit, specific government Departments were also charged with advancing policy change towards the wider goal of reforming the welfare system. An important plank in this overall policy is evident in the continuation (from Conservative to New Labour administrations) of American-inspired welfare-to-work policies which are the concern of this book. The influence of American thinking and policy examples is shown, for instance, in a visit to the US by members of the (parliamentary) Social Security Committee in December 1997. The resulting report identified common features of the two countries but also noted 'profound differences' in the health care and social security (income maintenance) systems of the two societies.

The Committee Report concluded that the key issues in need of consideration in the UK included: gaining support for welfare reform; assessing whether labour market changes were sufficient and of a kind to sustain a welfare-to-work approach; acknowledging concern about possible harm to children of pressuring lone mothers into work; and shifting the balance from passive benefits to 'active welfare.'[17] Continuity in policy thinking was also evident in a number of speeches by the first Minister for Welfare Reform in the new government, Frank Field (October 1997–July 1998); in evidence by Field and Harriet Harman to the Social Security Select Committee in February 1998, and in the Green Paper (issued in March 1998). In evidence to the committee in February 1998, Harriet Harman outlined the government's three-track approach to reforming welfare through its welfare-to-work policies, which she summarized as:

- helping people into work;
- ensuring that work pays; and
- modernizing the infrastructure which supports work.[18]

The Green Paper, *New Ambitions for our Country: a New Contract for Welfare*, set out proposals for policy development which clearly linked reducing poverty not through the benefits system but through employment. Apart from outlining reasons why the welfare state was in need of reform, the Green Paper heralded the government's intention to 'rebuild the welfare state around the work ethic: work for those who can; security for those who cannot.'

The Green Paper started from an assumption that four 'ages' of welfare can be defined:

1 Stopping outright destitution;
2 Alleviating poverty;
3 Preventing poverty; and
4 Promoting opportunity/developing potential.

Britain is considered in the Green Paper to be at the third stage, but aspiring to the fourth (a claim that is questioned in Chapter 5). In this context the proposed 'third way' of welfare reform would take the form of 'promoting opportunity rather than dependence' – language which sounds very familiar to a US audience- as against espousing privatization with only a residual safety net, or maintaining the status quo but with uprating of benefits. Policy change and programme provision would be based on eight key principles, of which 'importance of work' comes first, followed by 'new partnerships for welfare', but with 'continuing importance attached to welfare services', support for specific groups – 'disabled people', 'people in poverty', and 'the socially excluded', 'tackling fraud', and 'modernization.' Implementation and evaluation of welfare change was seen as a long-term programme with effects to be judged over a ten- to twenty-year period against 32 'success measures.'

Regarding responses to the Green Paper, it is possible to read into it motives other than simply reducing welfare expenditure (which had been a more overt ambition of government during the Thatcher years), and to identify attitudes and policies initiated under the Conservatives. These echo the attitude that the poor are to blame for their poverty and require people to take any jobs available; ignoring the very real problems of structural unemployment discussed in Chapter 3. They also fail to promote other policy options, such as strategies to develop work opportunities, that is, pursuance of active labour market policies as illustrated in the Scandinavian and German systems.[19]

Other concerns include the anxiety that programmes which promote a transition from dependency to independence through involvement in jobs which are socially useful will not be sufficiently promoted, or that other forms of contribution to society, such as volunteering in the community, will not be valued.[20] On the other hand, some feminists are concerned that the continuing sanctioning and expectations of women's unpaid activities as carers in the family will simply serve to perpetuate women's dependency.[21] However, there may be some evidence of more recent engagement with these concerns, and these are discussed later.

The Welfare Reform Bill was announced in November 1998 as concerned with pensions reform, welfare-to-work, and reform of the benefit system 'for those who need it most'[22] and was passed in 1999 as the Welfare Reform and Pensions Act. Under the new legislation, there is a single 'Gateway' to benefits for those of working age (as signalled in *A New Contract for Welfare: the Gateway to Work*). The welfare-to-work approach is being carried through in a number of different areas, each labelled, in similar vein to somewhat older American terminology, 'New Deals'. These have been progressively put into practice for young adults (18–24 years), disabled people, lone parents, partners (of unemployed people), unemployed adults over 25 years, and people over 55 years. Expenditure in the region of £5 billion pounds has been identified as 'representing by a considerable margin the new government's largest single public spending commitment'.[23] The New Deals in relation to young adults and lone parents are discussed further later in this section.

It is not clear how far the government's policy development in this field might have been informed by the findings of a study of 42 welfare-to-work schemes implemented under the Conservatives.[24] This identified very low proportions, and wide variations between the numbers, of people getting jobs as a direct result of participation in the previous schemes (only 2–28 per cent), and also dramatic differences in the unit cost of such schemes (ranging from £3 to £3,000 per participant). Whether schemes resulted in a net saving or a net cost to the public purse varied from £7,000 saving to an £8,000 cost per extra person in work.

EXPERIMENTATION

The importing of US welfare-to-work policies has been marked by a search for 'ideas that work', as demonstrated in the role which local programme design and experimentation is playing in both the US and the UK. Theodore and Peck suggest that the American example of state 'discretion in welfare-to-work policy design within a minimalist national framework' has informed a policy of local discretion in UK policy implementation.[25] This chimes with other policy developments emanating from the Social Exclusion Unit and a general favouring of 'devolution' by New Labour, relative to the centralizing tendencies evident in policy change under the Conservatives. Theodore and Peck also suggest that the New Deal programmes in Britain mark a departure from previous welfare-to-work schemes in two important ways. The first is the extent to which local partnerships and initiatives are encouraged, and the second is the more 'client-centred delivery model upon which the Gateway is based'. However, there are also continuities and indeed the previously implemented jobseeker's allowance 'acts as "a feeder" programme for the New Deal'.[26]

LOCAL MODELS OF PROGRAMME DESIGN

Theodore and Peck have identified six 'local models' of programme design, three from the US and three from the UK, 'frequently...cited as examples of "best practice" in the field'. These range from 'hard' (punitive or minimalist) policies aiming to get the most people into jobs in the shortest time (as in the Greater Avenues to Independence of GAIN Project, developed at Riverside, California) to 'soft' policies, concerned with the gradual reinsertion of individuals into the labour market, in the context of wider goals of community regeneration, described later in this chapter. Other examples given include the Wisconsin Works project, discussed in chapter 3 of this text, Project Match in Chicago, and the New Deal approach for 18–24-year-olds, as developed in the UK, for example, in the contrasting cities of Cambridge and Liverpool.

While child poverty alleviation is not a specific goal of this programme, some of the people in this age group (18–24 years) are parents of young children, and employment may be expected to pay better than benefits. Under the New Deal for 18–24-year-olds participants enter through a common 'Gateway' and are assessed as requiring short or longer term intervention. It is also assumed that 40 per cent of young people will secure unsubsidized jobs during this 'Gateway' phase and will not require additional support. Of the remaining participants some are regarded as 'job ready' and channelled in to the 'employer option'. Under this option a young adult takes a job in the private sector (or now also self-employment) in a fairly short period of time. Employers receive £60 per week subsidy for up to six months for employing the person, including offering in-house training or day release towards an approved qualification.

The other three options require potentially longer term measures. In the voluntary sector option participants train in a voluntary organization for up to six months and are also expected to attain an approved qualification. In the third option, the Environmental Task Force, participants can pursue basic education and training courses for up to a year while in receipt of financial support. The schemes illustrate how programme design and performance, while informed by the same objectives and overall approach, may impact differentially according to local conditions.

Major variables in these conditions include the nature of the local job market as well as demographic and socio-economic characteristics of the population. For instance, in the first year of the New Deal, Cambridge had a below average unemployment rate (2.6 per cent) and Liverpool (with a rate of 10.8 per cent) had more than double the national average. This affects both the scale and the potential 'success' of the schemes, with New Deal in Liverpool trying to place 6,487 claimants into jobs in the first year of operation, many of whom had special needs (2,208) or special problems (1,234). In contrast, the Cambridge scheme expected to place 936 young adults over a 12-month period, although the proportion of these who may have special needs or problems had not been estimated.[27]

Another group which quickly became the focus of attention were lone parents (mainly mothers) estimated at nearly a million people currently, caring for about 2m children and costing £10 billion in benefits.[28] Benefit cuts to this group early in the life of the new government (December 1997) provoked unrest among some New Labour Members of Parliament and voters and also an outcry from interest groups advocating for lone parent families. There was subsequently some backtracking through various measures announced successive Budgets. Additionally, the inclusion of lone parents (mothers) in the welfare-to-work scheme has been less harshly implemented in the UK than in the US, with some continuing support for the role of mothers in bringing up children, at least in the pre-school years. While lone mothers with children under five can choose to approach a 'personal adviser' about work (or training) opportunities they are not required to do so. From April 2001 it is proposed that lone parents with children under five must attend for a work-focussed interview as a condition of receiving benefit.

Views about maternal responsibility for child care, relative to views about working mothers, are very ambivalent in the UK, as reflected in an element of 'double speak' about women's caring and work responsibilities in government policies, particularly with regard to lone mothers. There has been a general assumption in feminist thinking that work is the route out of female dependency (on men or the state) and into full citizenship. As such, society as a whole should assist women with children to pursue work if they so choose. However, as discussed in Chapter 3, there has also been recognition of the different schools of thought about women's role within feminism[29] and about the different cultural norms affecting women of different classes and ethnic groups. As in other areas where uniform policies are a blunt instrument for regulating behaviour or affording opportunities for individuals in particular groups, uniform, prescriptive policies aimed at pushing lone mothers into paid work are likely to be inefficient and oppressive.[30]

Apart from the ongoing debates (in Britain and the US) about the possible effect on children of having working mothers, Duncan and Edward's recent study suggests that a distinction should be made between the expectations of women in different social contexts about their responsibilities to care for children relative to seeking work, or the balance between the two roles which some women try to achieve (sometimes through combining part time work with child care responsibilities). Their work points to the need both for flexible day care provisions and financial support measures to underpin the different choices which women make (including the need to support care by a relative where this is the chosen option), and the recognition that these choices are partly dependent on the nature of local labour markets and employment practices. Choosing to work does not necessarily mean an escape from poverty, and the development of social transfers (or a social wage) to assist with the cost of parenting has only recently come on to the British policy agenda, despite examples of this policy in other European countries.[31]

Lister has also identified the growing influence of an 'ethic of care' (promoted under the Conservatives), and the danger that this can be used to promote 'compulsory altruism' of women which, in turn, perpetuates economic dependence and 'is corrosive of women's full citizenship'. However, there is some concern about the lack of value attached to unpaid (and indeed paid) care, and the need to reward caring activities (carried out, in one sense, on behalf of society) or, at least, to acknowledge the citizenship rights of those involved in unpaid caring, through more developed conceptions of citizenship.[32] Lister's view that paid work represents the best route to economic well being and independence for women leads her to conclude that the welfare-to-work policy in relation to lone mothers is legitimate but must have safeguards for mothers of babies and young children, or children with disabilities, or those within the first year of separation.

Additionally, it must be supported by effective provisions in relation to 'adequate' child care; appropriate education, training and employment packages, and family friendly policies in the work place, though as Lister herself acknowledges, the UK is a 'long way from achieving the social and economic infrastructure' to support such a policy.

Some of the debate about the extent to which lone mothers wish to work centres on the deterrent effect of the costs of entering the labour market, where taxation or low pay may reduce their income to little more or even less than benefits would have provided, and the lack of security which entry into a flexible labour market entails, compared to the poor but stable circumstances of staying on benefit. To some extent the government has sought to address the disincentives of entering low paid work (not exclusively for lone parents) through establishment of a minimum wage and the introduction of working families tax credit.

In relation to the first, a minimum hourly wage (of £3.60 for people over 21 and £3 for 18–21-year-olds) was introduced from April 1999, amid expressions of concern by some employers that this would lead to increased unemployment (including through risks to financial viability of some businesses) but in the expectation that this would act as an incentive for some people to enter work rather than remain on benefits. It was also estimated that it would boost the earnings of about 2m existing employees by an average of 30 per cent. Two-thirds of these gains would go to households in the bottom fifth of income distribution.[33]

There was similar thinking behind the introduction of the working families tax credit which replaced an earlier Conservative attempt to support families in receipt of low wages by payment of family credit (introduced 1988) through the benefits system, but this had a relatively low take-up and was of no benefit to the poorest families where there was no working parent. It was initially estimated that the new tax credit (implemented from October 1999) would encourage 92,000 people to enter the labour market (apart from benefiting some already in it)[34] and benefit 400,000 families.[35] It is worth more than family credit was, and is channelled through the Inland Revenue (responsible for taxation) rather than the Benefits Agency. While this is intended to remove the stigma which receipt of benefits may carry, it may also affect the distribution of income within the family, although for couples it need not necessarily be paid through the wage packet and, in the case of dispute, could be paid to the parent who has the main care responsibility for children.[36]

Associated tax and National Insurance changes, also introduced under the 1998 budget, were similarly aimed at enhancing the income of low wage earners and encouraging entry to work.[37] While such financial incentives have been welcomed, there is a danger that insufficient attention is being given to other obstacles to entering the labour market (for example, housing or transport needs) which are now revealed as major concerns in the US as a result of local welfare reforms.

Another disincentive to entering work in both the UK and US, particularly for lone mothers, concerns the availability of affordable child care, and wider issues about child care provisions for children under school age and about care before and after school. In terms of financial support measures, a Conservative scheme to assist with child care costs has been replaced through the introduction of child care tax credit to cover 70 per cent of the costs of child care for children in low and middle income families.[38] A further initiative, which apparently recognizes both the needs of (young) people for training and the workforce implications of expanding the range of affordable child care, included the plan to train 50,000 people as child–care workers through the voluntary sector scheme, as announced in the Green Paper.[39]

The other area which can be briefly considered here, and which extends beyond addressing the needs of lone mothers, concerns the development of family friendly policies in the work place. In 1999 67 per cent of women and 84 per cent of men with dependent children were in paid employment (including over half of mothers with children under five years). A 1996 EU Directive on Parental and Family Leave, concerned with parental leave to care for young children and family emergency leave, had been largely ignored under the Conservatives but was due for implementation by 1999 and has been incorporated into the Employment Relations Act 1999. This is important in promoting improved rights and protection for people with care responsibilities, although, in so far as the provisions, including for parental leave, are largely unpaid, the extent to which they will benefit low income families is probably limited. Experience in Sweden, with a much longer record of parental leave, also suggests that this particular provision will do little to shift the established patterns of 'mother care' of babies and young children, with associated disadvantages to women in promotion terms, the longer the period out of work.

Other recent moves and statements suggesting government support for an extension to family friendly policies include the adoption of the EU Working Time Directive in 1999 which seeks to limit working hours overall and regulate some aspects of working conditions and a Consultation Document (January 2000) on implementation of the 1997 EU Directive on Part-time Work. However, in relation to the first, many employees remain under heavy pressure to work long hours (whether or not formally recognized in overtime pay) although in areas of work still unionized (despite significant reduction of union powers under the Conservatives), pressures to cut the working week to 35 hours have been given a boost by changes in French legislation on this matter since January 2000.[40]

With regard to the second point, one quarter of the work force (about 6 million people of whom 1 million are men) work part-time and the government intends to boost this number and improve general working conditions. Part-time work is particularly common in the retail and service industries as well as the hospital and social care sectors, and while there has been significant expansion in job numbers, 'most jobs remain low paid and low in status'.[41] Such staff may still lose out on promotion opportunities and/or important fringe benefits, and there has been criticism that, even in the Consultation document, part-time work is still regarded as a 'women's issue' and an important chance to expand employment opportunities has been missed. Part-time work is rarely available to people in more senior posts (despite experience and circumstances) and even the practice of 'flexitime', which might be found useful by lone parents or where both parents are working, applies to only a minority of employees.

Other measures which might benefit women and/or low income families include Maternity Leave, increased at the end of 1999 from 14 to 18 weeks and Parental Leave which was included in the recent legislation but is likely to be unpaid. Additionally, relatively few companies have arrangements (whether subsidized or not) for child care, or schemes for career breaks and retraining for parents returning after caring for young children or for others with care responsibilities.

There are of course, exceptions to this picture – which may have parallels in the US but can be compared unfavourably with some other EU countries, notably Scandinavia. But it is ironic that a trawl through the 1999 editions of *People Management*, which has previously included some interesting case examples of family-friendly policies in operation, produced only one example, related to the establishment of a work-based day centre for elder care. However, an article about improvement in working conditions in some call centres (a fast growing sector of the economy and major employer of women) suggested that a very low rate of staff turnover (1 per cent) at Littlewoods in Sunderland could be attributed to 'its family friendly policies' – which were not elaborated (though a cynic might ask whether there were other job opportunities available locally) and another example in Peterborough – a town with low unemployment rates – cited existence of a work place nursery as one of a range of measures to retain staff.[42]

It seems, therefore, that, despite much talk about family-friendly policies since the 1980s – and a more favourable political climate currently – actual developments in the UK still depend heavily on the policies of particular employers and, as such, improvements have so far been relatively marginal. In a particular area, recent mergers and technological changes in the financial services sector (including banking) have resulted in a reduction in the workforce and may have impacted on previous policies. Thus, at a time when the government is trying to boost employment opportunities and practices which support the family, there are concerns that there are insufficient incentives or sanctions on employers and that further developments might be limited by the competitive pressures of the 'global economy' on all companies.[43]

Turning to the effects of the welfare-to-work scheme to date, the Social Exclusion Unit (following its early role in investigating disadvantage and proposing new policies) has more recently acted as a monitoring agent for some of the changes. In this role, it has commented specifically on the differential rates at which people have benefited from employment opportunities through the government's welfare-to-work scheme, identifying disparities between the employment level of whites and other ethnic groups, and also the very poor record of employment among some women. It attributes these differentials to lack of skills and confidence as well as to discrimination by employers, rather than an overall lack of jobs, including in the areas where ethnic minority populations are concentrated. A recent report for the unit also identified a high level of 'invisible unemployment' among young people (16–24-year-olds) who were neither in work or education nor claiming benefit.[44] The implication being that many families in poor neighbourhoods (as well as the middle classes) are maintaining their children beyond the ages that might have been the norm a generation ago.

By 2000 the government could claim that over 250,000 people had started on New Deal programmes since they began in 1998, including many who had gained training and work experience with a view to entering permanent employment.[45] Moreover, more than 60,000 companies had signed New Deal employer agreements, but other policy changes along the way, in respect of lone parents and people with disabilities particularly, have meant that some people have viewed developments with a degree of caution, if not scepticism. At best, welfare-to-work schemes could be seen as assisting in combating discrimination against racial and ethnic minorities, people with disabilities and women (including lone mothers) in relation to entry to (or treatment in) the workplace.

They should also, however, include comprehensive safeguards so that people who are NOT able to access (or maintain themselves in) the labour market are not penalized with the knock-on effects felt by children in poor families.

NEW CHILDCARE AND PARENTING INITIATIVES, AND REDISCOVERING THE COMMUNITY

The Green Paper had 'tackling child poverty' as one of its principles. This included plans to increase child benefit, a universal provision, sometimes seen as the central cash benefit in the state's support for dependant children. However, this provision has declined in value significantly since its first inception as family allowance (established in 1946 and replaced in 1977), and was frozen completely for three years under Thatcher (from 1988 to 1990).[46] The value of child benefit has increased in the last three years, though it still contributes to only a small proportion of the total cost of raising children. A particular value of the benefit is that it is normally paid to mothers and has long been seen as a means of giving women control over at least a small part of the household income.

The government also planned to 'increase support to the poorest families', and announced a five year plan or National Child Care Strategy which would 'help 1 million children'.[47] Tellingly, one criterion against which progress would be measured in this area was a reduction in the number of children living in workless households. Previously identified concerns about the failings of the Child Support Agency were also addressed: the Green Paper noted that about one in three absent parents were still failing to maintain their children, but also that two in three mothers were trying to avoid claims against absent parents.[48] One of the criteria against which progress in this are would be measured would be an increase in the number of separated parents meeting their financial obligations. Finally the Green Paper identified concern about the rise in the rate of conceptions among girls under 16 and said that initiatives would be taken through the education system to address the problem, with improvement being assessed by a fall in the rate of (young) teenage pregnancies.

Other strategies identified in the Green Paper aimed to address social exclusion and raise health and educational standards and might also be seen to have an indirect effect on the current experience and future life chances of children in poor families. These strategies include an expansion in pre school provision, the establishment of after-school clubs, and the establishment of Health Improvement Programmes (HIPs) (some of which have been specifically targeted at children). The government, while resisting some calls to establish a Minister for the Family, did establish a Ministerial Group on Family Policy (under the Home Secretary) with a remit to see what could be done to improve the teaching of parenting skills and support for parents. A Consultation Paper, 'Supporting Families', issued later in 1998, signalled further the government's intentions. This paper considers developments in relation to teenage pregnancies, child care for children under five, and teaching of parenting skills and support for parents, it also looks at another strand in government policy relating to community development.

Policies in relation to 'teenage pregnancies' have recently been developed in response to the acknowledgement that, apart from the overall costs associated with the increase in lone parent families, Britain has the highest rate of teenage (under 17) pregnancies in Europe. In 1997 a draft Consultation Document was produced by the Health Education Authority outlining plans for a national strategy to reduce teenage conceptions. This then became an aspect of the work of the Social Exclusion Unit, and has since become a focus of attention in developing policies in the health and education fields.

The statistics in this field have to be viewed with caution since some relate to all teenage conceptions, that is, young people under the age of 20, who may then have an abortion (37 per cent of the 94,000 plus in this category in England and Wales, in 1996) or give birth at the age of 20. More specifically, in 1996, 9.4 girls in every 1000 under 16 became pregnant, a rate exceeded (among economically developed countries) only by the USA. However, there were wide geographical variations in this rate, which rose as high as 16.1 per 1000 in some inner London boroughs in the 1993–95 period.[49] A report by the Social Exclusion Unit in 1999 put the number of school age conceptions at 7,700 in 1997. A number of factors have been identified with higher risk of school age pregnancy. These include coming from low income families, large families, lone parent families or families from particular ethnic minority groups (Pakistani, Bangladeshi or Caribbean). Having witnessed domestic violence, been sexually abused, or being in public care also increased the risk.

A number of strategies to tackle teenage pregnancy and parenthood were recommended by the Social Exclusion Unit,[50] including a national public education campaign; increasing education and training opportunities for young mothers; more emphasis on prevention through sex education; and improvements in the preparation of both teachers and the Health Service in relation to preventive work and responses to pregnancy, birth and parenting needs. Additionally, the fathers of babies would be targeted to pay child support (through the CSA).

Changes to the curriculum proposed by the Department for Education and Employment tend to continue the earlier policy under which school governors have discretion as to whether 'sex education' is taught (and indeed there has been no change to the legislation pertaining to sex education since the 1993 Education Act). In these circumstances, it has sometimes been viewed as the responsibility of parents and therefore omitted, although imaginative programmes have been identified in some schools which address both the risks of early and unprotected sex and the consequences.[51] The overall approach in the UK contrasts sharply with, for instance, Dutch policies where the rate of teenage pregnancies is one of the lowest in Europe (6.4 per 1000) and where importance is given to both sex education in schools and public information.[52]

CHILD CARE

Despite the high level of mothers working (and others who would work if they could) alternative care for children under five in the UK is in short supply and the most expensive in Europe. A range of alternative care provisions can be identified, including nannies, au Pairs, and mother's helps (all unlikely to be options for low income families), day nurseries and child minders. In reality, child minders form an important element in child care provision, since they are seen as providing care more like the care that the child would receive in the home and may be more affordable than day nurseries. The latter may be provided by the local authority (but if so it is likely that most places will be taken by 'children in need', as identified under the 1989

Children Act) or by private companies, in which case the fees are likely to be beyond the purse of low wage earners. As already noted, company-sponsored day nurseries were encouraged under the Conservatives, a policy continued by New Labour, but, since nursery provision is seen as a taxable benefit (rather than a necessity for some employees), developments in this are have been at best, 'patchy', and, despite government rhetoric, there has been little real expansion of good quality, affordable day-care for children under five so far.[53]

There have, however, been government prompted initiatives in the form of additional support for young children in low income families and poor neighbourhoods, in both the pre-school and early years. These include the establishment of the Sure Start programme (1999–2002). This £540 million initiative, jointly sponsored by the Ministers for Health and Education, aims to establish 250 projects in (targeted) areas of social deprivation to work with parents and children under four. The stated goals are helping prevent family breakdown and promoting readiness for school.

The government has also announced the establishment of a £2.5 million Parenting Research Initiative, to be taken forward by the Department of Health, which of course, is also responsible for Personal Social Services. The Department of Health has advocated (since 1998) 'Refocusing Children's Services' on broadly based family support by local authority Departments of Social Services (away from an earlier pre-occupation with child protection) and it has been re-emphasized that local authority Children's Service Plans must take into account the provisions made by voluntary organizations, and work collaboratively with them in planning some of the new projects. Local authorities in partnership with other bodies have also been charged with producing Early Years Development Plans to provide good quality information to parents, to run pilot schemes that integrate the care and education of pre-school children and to ensure the contribution of parents to Early Excellence Centres which should be established around the country.[54]

One form of funding which has been drawn on for community based projects in relation to child care and parenting projects has been the Single Regeneration Budget (SRB). Local authorities, in partnership with other private and voluntary sector parties, have been able to bid for to improve provisions in run down areas. Shinman cites an example of funding from this budget being used to employ a Home Start worker in a neighbourhood where 68 per cent of children have free school meals. Home Start itself is an interesting example of an non-governmental organization established in 1973 to work collaboratively with schools and other neighbourhood services to support parents and facilitate school entry and attendance (largely through the use of local volunteers), which is now well placed to participate in funding applications and new projects.

The other area which is likely to be expanded further is the establishment of schemes closely tied into school and the education system. Examples include breakfast clubs and after school clubs. Both of these can be seen as extending the 'care' aspect of educational provision (and thus enabling parents to work), and after school play schemes are quite long established in some areas. The justification of breakfast clubs, (which are less in evidence) until recently was related to improving diets and thus children's ability to take advantage of the education offered (reminiscent of the justification for free school meals under the 1906 Act).

A recent study presents new research findings from Britain and the US about the importance of nutrition for children's development and looks at how breakfast clubs work.[55]

As far as the outcomes of the various new initiatives are concerned, it is too early for many of them to have been evaluated. However, in a recent reference to developments initiated under the Sure Start programme, the Minister for Education gave an example of a family literacy scheme run by a primary school on the outskirts of a former mining community in Stoke on Trent. Ten parents and children were recruited to the first family literacy scheme with reported improvements in children's literacy and parental involvement in their children's education.

There was no specific mention of whether this scheme improved the employment possibilities of the parents or financial circumstances of the family, but it does suggest a small step towards addressing another problem identified by a study carried out for government. This found that more than one in five adults have poor basic skills.[56] Another scheme described, based at the East Leeds Family Centre (but supported by local schools, colleges and university as well as local authority and local businesses), has apparently enabled over 2000 people in two years to improve their educational skills and opportunities, assisting in their return to education or transition into work. Both schemes, though clearly very different, suggest renewed attention to educational opportunities (in many forms and at different stages of life, as illustrated in the government's advocacy of 'Life Long Learning') as one route to 'breaking the cycle of poverty and welfare dependency'.

Perhaps one of the significant differences between New Labour and previous Conservative administrations is a new willingness to invest in the community and to allow experimentation in the implementation of new programmes at local levels to see 'what works'. Various statements emanating from government have declared the goal of 'empowering' people and communities (although such ideals have sometimes been juxtaposed against the evils of perpetuating passivity and dependency through the benefits system) and some have had specific goals with regard to neighbourhood improvement and community regeneration. By 2000, 18 Policy Action teams had been established focusing on key issues associated with the revival of poorest neighbourhoods.[57]

A recent growth in local food projects has also been cited as an example of community initiatives addressing local problems of poor health related to low income. A study by McGlone looked at 25 such food projects to see what had led to their establishment and what factors affected their success or failure.[58] Projects included examples of food co-operatives, community cafes, 'cook and eat' sessions and partnerships between retailers, local authorities and communities. While procuring and preparing nutritious food at low cost was usually a primary goal of such projects, there were often related 'spin offs' in terms of increasing individual confidence, extending social networks and improving community relations and expectations.

Returning to the New Deal programmes discussed earlier, the Wise Intermediate Labour Market (ILM) in Glasgow was identified as an example of a community based scheme at the 'soft' end of the continuum.[59] This scheme recognizes that the longer people have been unemployed the harder it is for them to re-enter the formal labour market and transitional arrangements and (re)training are needed to improve their prospects of employment. However, it goes further than this in linking the provision of jobs to a recognition that particular neighbourhoods also need regeneration and that work may have an important social (as well as economic) function for both individuals and communities.

The Glasgow scheme links a number of businesses providing work regenerating low income housing estates. It, therefore, has both job creation and training functions but in the context of improvement in the local environment and social economy. The scheme has many characteristics of the formal labour market – recruitment and selection procedures, wages and contracts – but employment opportunities are limited to the long-term unemployed and are temporary, providing a step on the way to employment in the formal labour market. The scheme varies from a number of other initiatives in operating on the principle of voluntary participation and having social/community goals as well as individually focused ones.

Evaluation of the outcomes for individual participants showed that their chances of employment in the formal labour market were significantly improved, with over two thirds finding jobs or being self-employed on leaving the scheme, although, in a city of higher than average unemployment rates, nearly half of these were unemployed again at a six month audit. However, for those who remained in employment, wage levels showed an improvement on jobseeker's allowance, and 'there was evidence of pay rises over time as participants move from the first job to subsequent jobs'.[60] While this account does not give any indication of the family status of the people employed in this scheme it can be assumed that some participants have children, and that additionally the improvement of local housing and facilities also benefits other children in low income families in poor neighbourhoods.

CONCLUSIONS: ADDRESSING CHILD POVERTY?

So what conclusions can be drawn from the foregoing discussion of recent policy intentions and implementation in the UK, with reference to the particular theme of addressing child poverty? This is but one aspect of the ambitious goals of the current government in relation to restructuring the social welfare system as a whole. Viewing these developments in the context of policy change during 19 years of Conservative government, and policy influences from both Europe and the US, there seems to be evidence of both continuity and change, and of influences from both continents.

Continuities with the previous government's policy are evident in some specific areas, for instance, in the attempt to shift financial responsibility for child maintenance on to absent parents, but other (and perhaps more effective) initiatives in relation to child poverty can be seen as part of wider aims and a new agenda to redress injustices in a society in which social divisions have become acute. The moral and pragmatic reasons for addressing economic disadvantage and other forms of exclusion have apparently gained recognition, and in this area, the influence of the EU seems significant. Conversely, the major emphasis being given to welfare-to-work policies (as a significant way of addressing inequalities at the individual level) apparently reflects US influence to a greater degree.

The means of curbing welfare expenditure and the achievement of such a goal thus continue to be through 'active welfare' policies, rather than through what has been termed a 'passive benefits' system. However, while clearly adopting a major approach from the US in the form of moving people off state support into work, implementation of this approach in the UK suggests some important differences, and takes place within a wider context of state social welfare provisions.

The welfare-to-work scheme has been given at least tacit support in many quarters, and has even been welcomed as affording improved opportunities to some groups whose ability to work has previously been impeded, but major concerns remain about the ability of the labour market to 'absorb' the number and range of people who may now be 'actively seeking work', particularly in some areas of the country where high unemployment rates are a long-standing feature. In these circumstances it seems that increased attention to macro economic factors and labour market policies, as is evident in the policies of some European neighbours, must accompany the attention which is being paid at micro level to individuals who are unemployed.

Differences in implementation between the UK and US are particularly marked in relation to lone parents where, despite similar concerns, the government is apparently reluctant to extend benefit sanctions to mothers of pre-school children. This may also be a tacit acknowledgement of the paucity of day care provisions for children under five and the recognition that 'parental care' (whether or not it is best for children and the parents involved) usually provides the cheapest form of care, even when parents are supported by state benefits. In the broader field of child care, the (somewhat confusing) array of recent initiatives which the government has encouraged to benefit children in low income families (whether one or two parent) tends to emphasize goals related to healthy child development and improved parenting skills although we are now seeing push for increased day care provision.

Overall, some other clear themes are evident in current policy moves, including a continued shift towards involvement of the voluntary and commercial sector in the provision of a range of social welfare schemes and a strong emphasis (usually a requirement) on partnership arrangements between the traditional providers (local authorities) in planning and development of new services. The emphasis on involvement of all 'stakeholders' has also been accompanied by attempts to break down the traditional rivalries between departments, whether centrally or locally, to ensure co-ordinated programmes which recognize the multi-faceted nature of poverty and social exclusion. Inter-agency (and inter-professional) work has become a clear expectation of many of the schemes funded.

Another major theme is the encouragement being given to 'experiment' and to develop schemes which are responsive to local conditions. While these have the benefit of flexibility, there is always some danger of territorial injustices arising, and the disadvantage that many schemes are funded on a pilot basis and may face an uncertain future at the end of particular initiatives. This is particularly true of schemes in the social welfare sector and poor neighbourhoods which aim to meet the needs of the least well off who, in some cases, may be poorly placed to contribute (whether materially or in kind) and may lack the skills to access support from other sources when initial funding has expired.

On a related point, to date there is less evidence in the UK of the 'support' (of various kinds) for individuals and communities by corporations which is evident in the US. However, this is clearly a growth area in relations to some aspects of 'welfare provision' for some individuals in the UK (for instance, though the inclusion of private pensions and health care insurance in some company packages to attract or retain senior or scarce staff) and this may become more evident at community level as some of the new programmes develop. Despite some recent improvements (partly owed to the implementation of European Directives), there seems little evidence so far that family-friendly policies operate at much more than a rhetorical level in most sectors of UK employment. Similarly, while there is some hope that implementation of a minimum wage will lift some families out of poverty, the establishment of the working families tax credit, also recognizes that many low wage earners still need assistance to raise their children.

So how realistic is the goal to halve child poverty in ten years and to eradicate it in 20? Two recent studies have looked again at the issue of children in poverty. The first interviewed children between the ages of 5 and 16 and gave their perspectives on the economic world around them and the implication of living in poverty for their own beliefs, behaviours and aspirations.[61] The second was based on secondary analysis of Family Expenditure Survey data and information from the National Child Development Study, and supported the argument that adults' economic and social positions, including their success or failure in the labour market, are linked to their experience of poverty as children.[62] Both point to the continuing need to target this problem specifically as well as devising programmes which address the wider environmental conditions in which poor children are raised.

It can be concluded that current government measures help improve the circumstances of some children in low income families, but there are continuing needs for investment in real jobs and in associated areas of support for parents and children, including training and re-training schemes, child care, and before- and after-school provision, as well as more (practical) encouragement of family friendly polices. (There are also other areas which have a bearing on employment opportunities, such as housing and transport polices which have not been considered here.) It seems unlikely that, even if the job market expands (or at least does not contract) and there are substantial improvements in the infrastructure to support parents working, self-sufficiency can never be assured in all circumstances, and some financial support provisions have to be retained and provided at a level which supports a decent standard of living. Some types of financial support measures can be justified as recognizing and valuing the contribution of people not in the waged economy, including lone mothers caring for children.

While experience in the US provides examples of policies which might be seen as offering both policy opportunities and warnings, some European (notably Scandinavian) examples do suggest that child poverty, (and indeed financial hardship experienced by other groups in the UK population) can be substantially alleviated by different societal expectations and arrangements. These include making personal provision through insurance schemes but also recognize collective responsibilities for some services and special circumstances through taxation. The idea that welfare provision should not be the sole prerogative of the state, but is reasonably a shared responsibility of statutory, voluntary, private and informal sectors, with individuals assuming greater responsibility for their own and their immediate family's care has now gained widespread acceptance in the UK. But there are continuing concerns about the need for equality of access to resources, including those which directly or indirectly address the needs of children and families experiencing poverty, and exclusion from opportunity. The challenge for the current government remains how to tackle this problem effectively.

NOTES

1 *Households Below Average Income*, 1994/5–1998/9, DSS, 2000.
2 S Shinman, *Strengthening Families to Build Strong Communities: Working Together*, Home-Start Report, Leicester, 1999.
3 J Hills, *Income & Wealth:the Latest Evidence*, Joseph Rowntree Foundation, York, 1998.
4 P Hall et al, *Change, Choice & Conflict in Social Policy*, London, Heinemann, 1975.
5 H Glennerster, *British Social Policy Since 1945*, Blackwell, 1995.
6 C Pollitt, *Manageralism and the Public Service*, Basil Blackwell, 1990. N Deakin, *The Politics of Welfare: Continuities and change*, Harvester Wheatsheaf, 1994.
7 J Ford, *Consuming Credit: Debt and Poverty in the UK*, CPAG, 1991.
8 M Freeman, *Children, Their Families and the Law: working with the Children Act*, Macmillan, 1992; C Pollitt, *Manageralism and the Public Service*. Basil Blackwell, 1990.
9 R Berthoud & M Ivacovou, Paytime, *Guardian*, 11/2/00.
10 M. Brooks, *Britain: New Labour's Tory's cuts, What lies behind 'Welfare to Work'*, 1998, http://www.lib.labournet.org.uk/1998/may/news11:html.
11 J McCluskey & C Abrahams (eds), *Fact File 1999*, NCH Action for Children, London, 1999.
12 A Goodman & P Johnson, *Inequality in the UK*, Oxford, Oxford University Press, 1997.
13 L Fox Harding, *Family, State and Social Policy*, Basingstoke, Macmillan, 1996.
14 R Lister, *Reforming Welfare around the Work Ethic: New Gendered and Ethical Perspectives on Work and Care*, Policy & Politics 27(2) pp223–246, 1999.
15 Green Paper, *New Ambitions for our Country: A New Contract for Welfare*, (3/1998).
16 R Deans, *Victimising the Victim*, 1998. www.lib.labournet.org.uk/1998/may/news11:html.
17 Social Security Committee report 1998, pp10–11.
18 Social Security Committee minutes, February 1998.
19 J Clasen & A Gould, *Long Term Unemployment and the Threat of Social Exclusion: A Cross National Analysis of the Position of Long Term Unemployed People in Germany, Sweden and Britain*, JFR & Policy Press, Bristol Unit, 1997.
20 B Jordan, *The New Politics of Welfare: Social Justice in a Global Context*, Sage, London, Thousand Oaks, 1998.
21 R Lister, *Reforming Welfare around the Work Ethic: New Gendered and Ethical Perspectives on Work and Care*, Policy and Politics 27(2) pp233–46, 1999.
22 A Darling, *Welfare Reform Bill will help meet the needs of the future*, 1998. www.mtgc.uk/co1/depts/GSS/co18399e.ok
23 N Theodore & J Peck, Welfare to Work: National Problems, Local

Solutions? *Critical Social Policy*, 19(4) pp485–510, 1999.

24 K Gardiner, *Bridges from Benefits to Work: a Review*, York Publishing Services for J.R.F.York, 1997.

25 Theodore & Peck, (note 23).

26 Theodore & Peck, (note 23).

27 Theodore and Peck, (note 23).

28 M Brooks, (1998) *Britain: New Labour's Tory's cuts. What lies behind 'Welfare to Work'*, http://easyweb.easynet.co.uk/-socappeal/welfare.html.

29 F Williams, *Social Policy: a critical introduction*, Policy Press, 1989.

30 S Duncan & R Edwards, *Lone Mothers, paid work and Gendered Mothers Nationalities*, Macmillan, Basingstoke, 1999.

31 J Lewis (ed), *Lone Mothers in European Welfare Regimes*, London & Philadelphia, PA, Jessica Kingsley, 1997.

32 R Lister, *Reforming Welfare around the Work Ethic: New Gendered and Ethical Perspectives on Work and Care*, Policy & Politics 27(2) pp233–46, 1999.

33 K Patel, (1999) 'Poverty' Wage set, *The Times Higher*, 17 September 1999 – citing research by the Low Pay Commission which now has responsibility to monitor the situation.

34 P Gregg, P Johnson & H Reed, *Entering Work & the British Tax & Benefit System*, London, Institute for Fiscal Studies, 1999.

35 A Marr, *Who's In: Who's out. Search*, Issue 30, 1998.

36 CPAG, *Welfare Rights Bulletin 143*, CPAG, 1998, p7.

37 P Gregg, S Harkness, & S Machin, *Child Development and Family Income*, York, Joseph Rowntree Foundation, 1999.

38 CPAG, The Working Families Tax Credit, *Welfare Rights Bulletin*, 143, CPAG, 1998, p7.

39 *Green Paper*, HMSO, 1998.

40 J Walsh, 'Head of Steam Builds Behind 35 Hour Week', *People Management*, 6 (4), 2000, p15.

41 A Alan, 'Shortsight', *People Management*, 6(3), 2000, p31.

42 A Hatchett, *People Management*, 'Ringing True', 6(2), 2000, pp40–42.

43 J Welch, 'Brown's childcare tax block fails parents and firms', *People Management*, 5(12), 2000, p11.

44 Wintour and Wazir, Job Schemes bypass Asians, *Race Issues in the UK*, Special Report 2000.

45 D Blunket, Empowering People & Communities for a Better Future, 2000. www.dfee.gov.uk/empowering

46 L Fox Harding, *Family, State and Social Policy*, Basingstoke: Macmillan, 1996.

47 *Green Paper* Summary, 1998.

48 *Green Paper*, 1998.

49 *Highlight No. 165, Parental & Families Leave*, NCB/Barnados, London, 1999.

50 SEU Report, 1999.

51 R WaterHouse, 'Too Much, Too Young?' *Guardian Education*, 14 September 1999.

52 *Highlight no. 165*, (note 49).

53 J Welch, 'Brown's childcare tax block fails parents and firms', *People Management*, 5(12) p11, 1999.

54 Shinman, 'Strengthening families to build strong communities: working together' *Home-Start Report*, Leicester, 1999.

55 N Donovan & J Street, *Fit for School: How Breakfast clubs Meet Health, Education and Child Care Needs*, New Policy Institute, London, 1999.

56 Moser Report, 'A Fresh Start: Basic Skills for Adults', DFEE, London, 1999.

57 Blunkett, (note 45).

58 P McGlone, B Dobson, E Dowler & M Nelson, *Food Projects how they work*, York, Rowntree Foundation, 1999.

59 N Theodore & J Peck, Welfare to Work: National Problems, Local Solutions? *Critical Social Policy*, 19(4) pp485–510, 1999.

60 Theodore and Peck, 1999.

61 J hropshire & S Middleton, *Small Expectations: Learning to be Poor*, York, Joseph Rowntree Foundation, 1999.

62 Gregg, (note 34).

5 Welfare policy that addresses child poverty: Summary and alternative visions for the 21st century

'A child in the United States is two or three times more likely to be poor than a child in a European country such as England, France, or Germany.'

Arloc Sherman, Children's Defense Fund, 1998

'I want the world to wake up. . . these women are worth the investment, and so are their children.'

Mary Kramer, 2000

Accomplishing true 'welfare reform' that reduces poverty and increases social inclusion is one of the most compelling goals of social policy for contemporary Britain and the US. Not only does successful reform open up the potential to free children from hunger or homelessness, it can give them different futures. As discussed in our Foreword and Chapter 4, welfare, state and reform are words which differ drastically in meaning depending upon which side of the Atlantic you reside. Such differences are also increasingly apparent according to which state of the US you live in. However, we maintain that reducing the numbers of children in poverty is the key measure of reform of income maintenance. In this conclusion we follow both the UK policy analyst Richard Titmuss and the US analyst Wilber Cohen for their adherence to the fundamental idea that: when, in countries of great wealth, many people, especially children, are poor, this is a failure of society and social policy rather than the people themselves.

It is clear that the UK is currently experiencing a pull in two directions. European neighbours are recognizing the dangers of increased inequality and exclusion, especially of children and teenagers, and are addressing structural issues, while the US continues to rely on encouraging or obliging parents to move from welfare to work. Politically it is persuasive to take the latter, narrower vision that poverty is the fault of lazy individuals, especially in the pre-occupation with avoiding increased taxation, and many parts of the policy arena collude with this tunnelled vision. In US medical research for child maltreatment, Theodore acknowledges that, 'the strong association between neglect and poverty makes it politically taboo (as a focus of study in medical journals), given the economic resources that would need to be invested to address the elements of poverty (associated with neglect).'[1] Yet, the wider structural view, while harder to sell politically, is socially and economically the only future for children. In the US, the McKnight Foundation has published a progress report on welfare reform, covering a number of the issues raised in Chapter 3. In the report a worker for a housing partnership speaks out:

> We work with a lot of people who are sometimes called 'high risk' or 'multiple-barrier' populations, these families need a different approach. The stick or the club doesn't work. Sanctions are pointless. You need to meet them where they are...I want the world to wake up, we realize that we work with the people with some of the hardest circumstances to overcome. It takes lots of personal attention and persistence and creativity. But these women are worth the investment, and so are their children.[2]

As we try to 'wake-up', we now focus on alternative possibilities for the new millennium. This chapter includes a summary of positive and negative factors of US policy (see figure 5.1). Also it identifies which aspects of US income maintenance policies are incompatible with UK social welfare goals; the key tensions and hazards that need to be publically discussed; why the media attention to 'successes' has captured the UK Cabinet; and what can be learnt from the current implementation and exercises in 're-framing' the concept of 'welfare.' We conclude by contrasting fears that the numbers of destitute will expand in the US as the cut off date of 2002 approaches, with visions of what could be different for children in this new century (see figure 5.3).

Before reviewing the positive and negative factors identified in figure 5.1, we need to recognize that three key tensions complicate the analysis of welfare reform and our attempt to apply current learning to future policy design. One of the most obvious is the *values conflict*

FIGURE 5.1: **Positive and negative factors in US Welfare Reform**

We have seen that the positives of US style welfare reform in relation to consequences for children include:

- public awareness of child poverty;
- promotion of public/private partnerships to help transitions into jobs with a living wage;
- recognition of the realities of shifts in employment patterns; and
- development of a profile of the 'family-friendly' employer, especially in terms of provisions for children, such as sick leave.

We have noted the following negative factors which affect children and their families:

- the current popular drift towards seeing work as the only solution without attention to the inadequacy of the minimum wage or pressures of parenting;
- lack of choice or financial support for people in poverty and little recognition of developmental benefits of caring for children under three in the home;
- political rhetoric concerning fraud (of a few) and dependency resulting in stigma, exclusion and alienation rather than participation and opportunity; and
- the media response to public sentiment, continuing to define welfare as a question of morality rather than social obligation.

---

between formal approaches of research and government reports and the public dialogue represented by some of our media. Stark figures and research concerning child poverty are available but remain spectacularly invisible in the political arena where public discourse often focuses more on alleviating dependency than ending poverty. A second tension is in the *challenge for politicians to engage the 'haves' in recognizing that income maintenance is part of the common good* and related to structural conditions and healthy, non violent communities, as well as to individual opportunity. A third tension is an *over simplification of the 'welfare-to-work solution'*.

VALUES CONFLICT

Public dialogue reflected by the media often skims the surface of what causes poverty and relies on myths about people experiencing poverty to interpret what is real, rather than facts and research reports which may challenge such values. As an example of value conflict between formal research and media messages, the report of the Centre on Budget and Policy Priorities points to the lack of connection between economic growth and a reduction in child poverty. Larni and McNichol in the Centre's study state:

> The robust economic growth (in the US) in recent years has done little to turn around the long-term trend toward increasing inequality...when similar points in the economic cycle are compared, it becomes clear that economic growth has been of, by and for higher income families...[3]

It would seem that a time of economic success and optimism would be the most likely period for poverty to be relieved, and for 'robust growth' to signal that the general public can afford to support those who are not sharing in the general increase in fortunes. Ironically, many people believe in the idea that a rising tide raises all boats, but the formal picture of income gains suggests that only the luxury vessels benefit.

A similar situation exists in the UK: the expansion of salaries in the upper income brackets has outpaced the increase in real incomes for families in poverty. Joe Rogaly, in his last column for the *Financial Times*, identifies the shifting values in relation to human well-being versus accumulation of wealth:

> Capitalism, science and technology, the three super stallions of the new millennium are careering out of control, dragging us into the unknown. For the upper crust of our species, this is the mother and father of all adrenalin rushes. Every day, it seems, there is a new electronic gadget, a further laboratory wonder, another genetic marvel...it is time to reflect on some of the fundamental changes in what is going on inside our heads. The big one is that our masters have finally decided that wealth creation is the greatest good, the prime objective of human endeavour. You can tell this from the hardening of attitudes to the poor.[4]

Furthermore, the current government statistics on disparities in wealth indicate a growing population excluded from participating in the economic growth of the privatization years. Even given a robust economy, skilled, technologically able, flexibly trained people will be more secure than those without skills or education. Indeed a study of the effects of welfare reform in the US indicates that those parents with basic qualifications who are able to leave welfare and depend on work to raise their children 'tend to have fewer children, a decent work history and a high school diploma.'[5] When the economy slows down and time limits on benefits expire, parents without skills or education will suffer most along with their children, as stated in the US Center on Budget Policy priorities report:

> As the new welfare law is fully implemented, more low-income recipients will face time limits and loss of cash assistance. Low-income families will be in particular danger during an economic downturn when lower-skilled workers will be the first to lose their jobs...

In the US, the statistics on the numbers of children enduring poverty are plainly available. According to the Children's Defense Fund and government reports, approximately seven million children are already members of families receiving income maintenance, and 14 million are members of families at or below minimum wage.[6] The President of Bread for the World, L Engelhardt, is unequivocal in his response to the welfare reform legislation: 'More than ending welfare as we know it, this bill will create hunger as we've never seen it. Most of the country's charities and religious bodies opposed this bill. The politicians have done what they think the voters want. But in several years when the devastating effects of this bill become fully apparent, decent people will be horrified.'[7]

Existing without enough food, without adequate clothes in winter and experiencing frequent bouts of ill health and childhood diseases such as asthma, are described by Bane and Weissbourd, as the 'quiet problems' of children. They make no noise. They storm no barriers, for now. The real tragedy is the loss of potential and the way healthy lives are put in jeopardy through persistently ignoring basic needs:

> As lower income families fall beneath the poverty line, even for short time periods, children will increasingly encounter a more pervasive set of 'quiet problems.' More children will come to school hungry, poorly clothed, and deprived of sleep because of overcrowding and inadequate heat. Additionally, more children will be debilitated by asthma, hearing and vision problems, obesity and accidental injuries.[8]

Policies that punish parents for not working in reality punish children. Physical discipline of children and adults has been challenged for years in development and corrections research.[9] Countries such as Sweden have outlawed corporal punishment and Norway has assigned an Ombudsman for Children. Jamaica has begun to model its children's services on the Convention on the Rights of the Child. Punishment is seen as counter-productive, it models negative behaviour, it produces resentment, it perpetuates the situation (of poverty, violence, exclusion etc). However, the US Welfare Reform system of sanctions amounts to harsh consequences for children. When even the barest minimum income is cut off, children are the first to suffer.[10]

Faber and Mazlish in their research and book 'How to talk so kids will listen and listen so kids will talk' identify the keys to motivation and change as choice, respect, listening to needs and role modelling.[11] Goleman, in his work on emotional intelligence, would assert that these are essential in the process of motivation for adults as well.[12] We can learn from countries which have provided for basic adult and child's needs and then address the questions of work and employment inside or outside the home. The US emphasis on sanctions is already being questioned and has resulted in the Children's Defense Fund Study of consequences, entitled *Welfare to What?* As the year 2002 approaches, the harsh consequences for children of sanctions and cut-off policies will be harder to avoid. In Minnesota alone, the 'Legal Services Advocacy Project estimates that about 12,000 families with 25,000 children will face an aid cut-off by 2003.'[13] By 2003, the US will be in direct disregard of the United Nations Convention on the Rights of the Child, Article 27, number 1: 'State parties recognise the right of every child to a standard of living adequate for the child's physical, mental, spiritual, moral and social development' (see Appendix 3).

While the reality of children trapped in poverty cannot easily be ignored, negative images of people in poverty as expressed in press reports, commentaries, cartoons and letter pages, threaten to focus attention elsewhere. A recognition of these distracting messages is a critical component in addressing social policy. For example, the cartoons of the first weekend in August, 1998, in the UK Sunday papers were both shocking and compelling. An image of Frank Field, former Minister for Welfare Reform, slowly swinging on a hangman's noose made an indelible imprint in its representation of the vituperative exchanges that last week of July 1998 in the UK Parliament. These exchanges labelled efforts at welfare reform as too costly, too long coming and unrealistic, and pilloried reformers as out of touch and spendthrift of taxpayers monies. How can the welfare debate have engaged such extreme and wrenching emotion? Examining the tensions reflected in these events sheds light on the limits and opportunities for welfare reform as an anti-poverty strategy. Policy makers can help to direct public attention to the benefits of alleviating poverty rather than exaggerating the supposed harms involved in being dependent on public assistance.

For Patricia Hewitt, in a response to Frank Field's Green Paper, the need for a new type of policy in this new millennium is clear:

> We want to break the cycle of dependency and insecurity, and allow everyone in Britain to lead a dignified life...Welfare has three key failings. First, problems of inequality and social exclusion are getting worse...people on welfare face barriers and disincentives in returning to work and fraud is seeping money away from genuine claimants... Reform must be guided by principles, as well as pounds. This is not just an issue of cash...if you set out to save money by dropping rolls, you end up spending more...[14]

Hewitt's notion of a welfare state is the comprehensive British version, outlined in the Foreword. It follows, for her, that 'welfare reform' is more about the health of the entire population: 'Welfare is about health, about schools, about social services...it is about active assistance into work. It is about promoting opportunity...not only do we all pay for the welfare state, we all benefit from it too.' This last principle, which recognizes the collective benefit of welfare provisions, is one of the most elusive in the political and public arena. There is a stubborn resistance to this idea from those who seek tax limits, cuts and rebates, even in the face of the obvious threats to health, education, employment opportunities and well resourced communities.

GETTING THE MESSAGE ACROSS ABOUT INCOME MAINTENANCE

It may be more than politics which prompts this resistance to seeing the common ground in welfare reform. At issue in the second tension, *engaging 'the haves' in recognizing structural elements of child poverty*, is the idyllic image of a former, more glorious age of managing meagre means and working for what you received. For example, in a much more constrained and challenging interpretation of welfare reform than Hewitt's, Lord Harris reminds us of the changing values surrounding thrift. His article was prompted by the discovery of his mother's insurance policies upon her death. They seemed meagre from a contemporary viewpoint, but they represented her hard work, planning, saving and concern to be responsible:

The dual debasement of public money and private thrift through inflation and unbridled state welfare have made a mockery of ingrained habits of self-help...It was the sight of her shrunken bequest that rekindled my anger with politicians of all parties...they have undermined prudent self-help through the three spiralling mischiefs: ceaselessly debauching the currency, exploiting the resulting anxiety as a vote-winning pretext for extending state welfare, and finally financing spending by extending the reach of income tax and thereby entrenching dependency at the expense of self-help...costs rising in the corrosive moral damage caused by a spread of wilful irresponsibility far beyond the formerly independent working classes.[15]

Certainly, as discussed in Chapter 3, it is crucial to review the policies which address fraud and persistent avoidance of employment opportunity for single, able-bodied people. However, the question for Lord Harris remains: has he tried to raise children on public assistance? His mother managed, but at what toll, and should others now, when the possibilities are so much greater and the wealth of the few so extreme, be required to repeat the harsh realities of the depression of the 1930s?

Ironically, while welfare debates have a familiar ring in both the US and the UK, there is one significant difference: the US economy of the twenty-first century is booming. There is a shortage of labour, and the current winning argument is that people have every opportunity to work and should be doing so. A senior executive of the international company, Dairy Queen, tells the familiar and popular story of working for what you get:

The way to be a 'have' instead of a 'have not' is to work and save: Lately I have seen a number of articles in this paper regarding the differences between those who 'have' and those who do not...I am in the group editors refer to as the 'haves' but that wasn't always so. I'm sure my story of success, in one way or the other, is reflected a million times over in the lives of others who fit into that category. My life has been characterized by long hard hours of study and work...I focused on my education while working as many as three jobs at one time – most at minimum wage and without much glory...Along the way I saved a little money here and there. I didn't buy what I couldn't afford. When I went to work at my first 'big job' I took on a troubled company. I worked as much as 100 hours a week. I am growing weary of criticism levelled at economically successful people and organizations. Increasing numbers of people across all lines of race, capability and means are becoming economic success stories every day. They are not to blame for those who try and don't do as well, or who make deliberate choices about lifestyles...[16]

The key point raised by Broin is: that there are those who are deserving and those who are not. He considers himself deserving in a way most of us would hope to be, because of hard work. Then the questions arise: who enabled him to be deserving within his nurturing system; and how is it possible for example, to work for 100 hours a week and raise children (the role of women for most of this century)? How can social policy be incarnated in a way that harnesses the motivation of the 'haves' to mentor and sponsor those experiencing poverty rather than producing the weariness or defensiveness Broin expressed? Why is it that some 'haves' recognize that people, particularly women with children, may be 'have nots' because of social arrangements and discrimination as well as their own choices; while others do not consider themselves in any way to be responsible for the plight of others? And crucially, children are innocent in this saga, and we are seeking a way to support their families without judging them as less deserving because of a different life pathway.

OVER-SIMPLIFICATION OF THE WELFARE TO WORK SOLUTION

The third tension which makes welfare reform so complex is the over-simplification in the US of the welfare-to-work solution. Georgia's WorkFirst welfare reform programme published initial results in November 1998. The number of parents moving from welfare to jobs was seen as encouraging; however, the bad news for children was that families were mainly entering the lowest paid sectors of the workforce:

> A welfare recipient reaches an economically viable milestone if he/she was paid more than minimum wage for full-time employment extending over a period of nine months. For the 15-month period studied, 39.2 per cent were employed for three consecutive quarters after exiting WorkFirst. However, only 14.2 per cent of those were earning more than minimum wage for full-time service.[17]

Studies in 1999 and 2000 for Minnesota and Ohio reflect the same trend as Georgia:

Ohio may be cutting its welfare rolls, but a new study says the state is doing a poor job of actually reducing poverty, especially among children…Nearly one-fourth of all Ohio children continue to receive some form of public assistance; in Cuyahoga County, the figure is one-third, according to the figures.[18]

The UK term 'workpoor' could apply to the outcomes described in this study. Achieving employment full-time, organizing the child care necessary for a family with young children, working and travelling long hours, establishing work habits, but earning less than the minimum wage, do little for children.[19]

FIGURE 5.2: **Factors in Successful Transition to a Living Wage**

BARRIERS	OPPORTUNITIES
Age: teenage parent or midlife	Age: young adult (25-35)
Education: without qualifications	Education: high school diploma
Dependents: two or more children under five or child with disability	Dependents: one, over 2 years, not disabled
Language: English as second	Language: English first
Housing: market for affordable housing shrinking.	Housing: access to established, long-term affordable housing.
Transport: dependent on public service	Transport: owns a car.
Social supports: isolated or threatened violence.	Social supports: network of kin & friends
Health: (including mental and drug related) services limited	Health: well, not addicted, services available.

The most recent US studies consistently show that while many parents prefer work to welfare, the wages earned by parents who have moved from welfare to work under pressure are around $7.50 (£5.00) per hour (about half what is needed to raise children) and few are in jobs that include health care coverage. Transport from where families live to where jobs are located is inadequate, as is child-care provision. Also parents facing the multiple challenges of mental health, disability, violence, alcohol and drug dependency are not managing effectively without welfare supports. The number of homeless families continues to rise in the US. The need for government intervention and safeguards against the negative impact on children of parents working full-time on low wages is not easily questioned.

What initiative the US or UK is willing to support is altogether another matter. As the European Union moves towards establishing a minimum wage, the question becomes one of how the support of families with young children can be re-framed as the building of healthy communities, by-passing the reactions of wealthy people feeling 'blamed' or the impressions of the general public that people experiencing poverty are a drain on resources.

US-style welfare reform is clearly punitive; if the recipient does not comply with work regulations soon enough, sanctions result and parents lose benefits, a direct consequence of which is the hunger and potential homelessness of children. Obliging people to take low-paid employment simply perpetuates the poverty of children even though it may make the welfare rolls look good. Certainly some families respond well to the pressure to seek employment and these are obviously the ones used as publicity for the 'New Deal for Lone Parents'.[20] However, for others the policy is a downward spiral to deeper exclusion from society. A profile could be developed which would indicate the families for whom work and a personal adviser are most likely to be successful, by assessing the risk factors and opportunity factors for successful transition to a living wage, such as figure 5.2.

Unpeeling the layers of belief about poverty is a necessary though complex process. There are constantly recurring themes of advantage and disadvantage, particularly in response to US style welfare reform which can help focus the evolving UK policy to a more direct application to children's poverty. These themes are explored below.

POSITIVE ASPECTS OF US STYLE 'WELFARE REFORM'

PUBLIC AWARENESS OF CHILD POVERTY

The most outstanding feature of the 'welfare reform debates' has been the raising of public dialogue. The years 1998-2000 will be remembered as years of constant conversation concerning issues of poverty — constant in terms of the level of media attention, parliamentary debate and party political platform discussions. In the US the new legislation prompted town meetings, tours around the country by Senators such as Paul Wellstone, revised worker orientation, agency renewal. Interest in poverty has been revitalized and new people have entered the field. In some ways the 'welfare reform' experiment has been reminiscent of the work in Britain in the 1980s concerning de-institutionalization. At that time, David King, Director of the Exeter Health Authority, spoke eloquently of the need for towns and villages to come together to discuss their fears, concerns and hopes for the 'new' legislation to include the excluded (in this instance, the mentally ill and vulnerable). His authority's film, 'Peace of Mind,' and the evaluation reports 'Tell Them Thank You' relate a story of public education in relation to mental illness. When income maintenance recipients tell their story, it becomes easier to understand the realities of life 'on benefit' and to see that such an existence, relying on minimal public income maintenance or being required to work at minimum wage which means placing very young children in day care, is not a lifestyle many would choose and is not conducive to optimal child development.

PROMOTION OF PUBLIC/PRIVATE PARTNERSHIPS

A number of politicians in the current Labour Government, as well as the cross-party Select Committee discussed in Chapter 4, have placed the British public on alert that welfare reform is about more than government intervention and that it casts a wider net to society as a whole. The wider cast is not only in terms of raised awareness, but also in terms of practical action. Such action is focused especially on public-private partnerships, and in this regard, the UK has much to learn from the US. There are a number of companies in the US who have accepted their social responsibility and who are crucial in facilitating the transition from welfare to work. The Xerox Business Services' efforts to support welfare recipients returning to the workforce were discussed in Chapter 3, and there are increasing numbers of organizations who are supporting transitions and initiatives including non-profit organizations who offer job counselling services and access to lower priced housing and car loans as bridges to self sufficiency.

For the UK, the history of social policy suggests that bringing private enterprise into the field of poverty is a contradiction. Private enterprise represents a profit motive: the ultimate goal is to make money rather than to offer service. Human service and social policy are usually based in concern for the common good, rather than making money from human problems. However, there is a need for re-thinking this traditional separation; such partnerships may offer a collective power to make policies more effective. Dayton Hudson, a US exemplar of corporate social responsibility, is one of the more enduringly successful companies. Their retired chairman stated: 'A management that's thoroughly involved in its community is better equipped to anticipate and manage change.'

RECOGNITION OF REALITIES OF SHIFTS IN EMPLOYMENT PATTERNS

The US report Workforce 2020, is unequivocal in its emphasis on skilled workers, workers comfortable with technology and prepared to be flexible during their lifetimes. In the US, welfare reform has been universally claimed as 'back to work' legislation. Both formal reports and the media have focused on the work component as central (rather than education, or child care or re-framing women's work in the home). Many states have assessed their policy success according to falling rolls, assuming that people have resolved their poverty issues if they are back in the workforce. If they have not complied with the state regulations concerning job search the sanctions discussed in Chapter 3 are imposed regardless of the consequences for their children. These sanctions are getting more severe and it has been suggested that 'the logic of tougher measures is like calling a guillotine a health-care device.'[21]

Ironically, the emphasis on getting people back to work may be a short-term solution; the lack of emphasis on education and training opportunities is a major flaw that will become more evident as the predictions of the Workforce 2020 report come into effect. Low wages, supported by the instant availability of people re-entering the workforce, present a major barrier in raising people with children above the poverty line. Low paid, unskilled jobs are also vulnerable to economic fluctuations, regional and global shifts of markets in a way that is vividly portrayed by J J Wilson in his research *When Work Disappears*.[22] One positive element concerning employment is the increased scrutiny that has come about as a result of the welfare reform legislation, as states work to track their recipients and to support job search and job counselling needs.

DEVELOPING PROFILE OF THE 'FAMILY FRIENDLY' EMPLOYER

The Midland Bank discussed in Chapter 3 was perhaps the exemplary family-friendly employer in the UK. Ironically, the bank has been taken over by the Hong Kong Bank and the economic frailty of social policy has been underscored as the new bank focuses on profit rather than being family-friendly. Other initiatives exist of course, including the collaborative regeneration schemes in Glasgow highlighted in Chapter 4, but the levels of bank policy that were addressed by the Midland are helpful in setting the objectives for employers at the individual level, the family, community and the corporate level. There are extensive opportunities for employers to expand their policies in relation to families, and the high proportion of lone parent families within the welfare reform picture means a pressure on employers to respond to their needs. The distribution of family-friendly businesses is still extremely uneven in the US, and marginal in the UK. There are examples, however, that can be highlighted as exemplary and encouraging to organizations that see the potential in a diverse workforce (see Appendix 1).

CONCERNS WITH US STYLE WELFARE REFORM

THE DRIFT TOWARDS SEEING WORK AS THE ONLY SOLUTION WITHOUT ATTENTION TO THE INADEQUACIES OF THE MINIMUM WAGE

As mentioned above in relation to wider understanding of the demands of a technology driven marketplace, there are many elements in tackling welfare reform of which work is only one, albeit an important part. Elements such as transport, access to training and higher education, housing, child care, healthcare, acknowledgement of the camouflaged occupational welfare of able-bodied middle class women, dignity of work in the home, programmes for the prevention of teenage pregnancy and recognition of housework and taking care of your own children under five as 'work'. While Chapter 3 addresses these elements in detail, two themes dominant in the lives of children and in the literature concerning welfare reform are revisited here: transport and higher education.

Contrary to popular myth, the majority of people receiving income maintenance from government sources are not lazy, fraudulent, able-bodied adults but lone parents and young children. In addition to the challenges of raising a young family on meagre income, there are some very practical barriers to retaining work including transport.

In a study of vehicle ownership and transport barriers, Pawasarat and Stelzer found that: 'The difficulties of getting to the child care provider, then to work, back to the child care provider and home contribute to job retention problems.' The Department of Transport's driver license files and vehicle records were compared with the welfare status of 93,908 individuals in Milwaukee County. Records showed that only 3.3 per cent of individuals expected to work owned a car, expanding to 12 per cent when family members in the household are included. The researchers concluded: 'Single parent women with children under the age of six had much higher employment levels when there was a car in the household'.[23]

Current or recent welfare recipients as car owners   1998 US

full-time employment	part-time employment
42% of car owners	16% of car owners
12% people without a car	11% people without a car

(John Pawasarat, Frank Stetzer, Removing Transportation Barriers to Employment: Assessing Driver's License and Vehicle Ownership Patterns of Low-Income Populations. University of Wisconsin-Milwaukee Employment and Training Institute, July 1998 & http://www.uwm.edu/Dept/ETI/dot.htm)

For the UK, public transport is often more readily available than in the US. However, in rural areas and when accompanying more than one child, privately owned means of transport is one of the keys to maintaining work while raising children. The supports for transport are particularly controversial in the US with the tensions between rural and urban needs. The McNight report supports a longer term emphasis on public services: 'Car loans, while a good solution for some participants, are not feasible for all participants. More viable, long term transportation solutions are needed for people without cars.'[24]

In relation to higher education, we see repeated references to the low educational qualifications of many welfare recipients. The UK Focus Files inform us that many parents are without basic credentials and the Moser Report identifies the need for resources to increase the basic skills of adults experiencing poverty.[25] The connection between education and a living wage is a close one, but has been ignored in the funding streams of the US Welfare Reform legislation. During the 1998/99 academic year, welfare recipients who were also students lobbied their legislators about the lack of support for their educational interests and needs in the legislation and implementation process. Welfare reform provisions had repealed earlier programmes supporting enrolment in higher education as an option to prepare for gainful employment in a number of states, including Minnesota. The rationale for these repeals was that work is a better training for maintaining a job than college. Amendments are now being offered in Minnesota to re-instate positive language and funds supporting at least two years of college as an appropriate option for employment training for some clients.

In Chapter 4, Lyons refers to Harriet Harman's outline of the UK government's three track approach to reforming welfare through its welfare-to-work policies:

- helping people into work;
- ensuring that work pays; and
- modernizing the infrastructure which supports work.

It is now clear in the US that the first step should be the infrastructure, rather than the push to being in work without recognition of the consequences of putting work at any price before skills training, education and family supports. We know that low-skilled and part-time work does not pay enough to keep families with children out of poverty and the recent University of California-Berkeley and Yale report, *Remember the children*, reported the following findings:

- Young children are moving into low-quality child care settings as their mothers move from welfare to work.
- Young children's early learning and development is limited by uneven parenting practices and high rates of maternal depression.
- Child care subsidies reach unequal factions of poor families and encourage the use of unlicensed care. The share of women drawing their child care subsidy ranged from just 13 per cent in the Connecticut sample to 50 per cent in Florida.[26]

A profile of the families for whom welfare-to-work policies are currently effective is developed on figure 5.2. However, policies which require hasty transition to work by lone parents create problems for children. This same report identifies increased depression of mothers under pressure and the lack of time for simple activities, such as reading at bedtime, all of which contribute to the steady drip of *quiet problems* for children.

LACK OF CHOICE, FINANCIAL SUPPORT AND RECOGNITION OF DEVELOPMENTAL BENEFITS OF CARING FOR CHILDREN UNDER THREE IN THE HOME OR IN SMALLER NURTURING CHILD CARE

A key to helping families thrive is the availability of affordable child care in settings which provide the attention of in-home care and flexible arrangements for the very young child. While corporations are increasingly turning their attention to the provision of child care, it is clear that those families receiving subsidies and able to maintain stable child care arrangements are those whose employment patterns are most settled and successful. Pawasarat and Quinn write of the Wisconsin experience:

> High turnover and high volume patterns of child care appeared to mirror the employment experience of many new entrants to the labour force, flooding the Milwaukee County payment and regulatory system with thousands of short-term child care placements. Previous analysis of employment patterns for AFDC recipients showed that 75 per cent of new hires in second quarter of 1996 failed. Similar patterns can be seen in the consistency of care for children in day care settings where 69 per cent of new care placements subsidized by Milwaukee County in the first half of 1996 failed to last into 1997.

Those few families able to maintain consistent care for their children had the characteristics of those most likely to remain off AFDC (income maintenance) and hold sustained employment. Placements of children in low-income non–AFDC child care settings were tracked for sixteen weeks in February 1996 and February 1997. The parents of children who had consistent care for sixteen weeks were better educated (85 per cent had 12 or more years of schooling) and most (68 per cent) had a driver's licence; 75 per cent of the children in consistent care were aged four or older.[27]

Clearly the availability of affordable child care is a major aspect of welfare reform when we see that over seven million welfare recipients are children.[28] However, there are at least two ironies accompanying the preference for full-time, outside the home, work as the answer:

(i) caring for and raising healthy children involves work in the home;
(ii) government reports in both the US and the UK confirm that children under three develop and thrive when their primary caregiver (particularly for children under two) is a parent or extended family member.

These two issues highlight the contradiction of requiring a parent to work full-time *outside* the home and pay for another person to work at raising their young children with no choice as to the possible combinations which would benefit both parent and child. The arguments relating to choice and the feminization of poverty are particularly relevant here; lone parents are overwhelmingly women and they need the range of options that are currently the preserve of men.[29]

Instead of restricting choice, which is the focus of the current US welfare legislation, revised legislation in the UK could open opportunities for parents to choose whether to work outside or in the home and in combinations of both. Raising their own children and having formal recognition of this category of '*work*' while also having the choice to work part-time outside the home with subsidized childcare, or to enter training and further education is a powerful combination for strengthening families. Currently, this sort of flexibility is available in a number of EU countries, such as Denmark and Italy, but not yet in the US or Britain. The current interest in 'joined up' thinking in Britain, however, may lead to greater co-ordination of policy in terms of such flexibility. At present the Department of Health and Education Minister's concern with 'refocusing children's services' appears to leave out employers and policies which recognize work in the home.

POLITICAL RHETORIC ABOUT FRAUD AND DEPENDENCY PUSHES PEOPLE FURTHER INTO THE EXCLUSION AND ALIENATION RATHER THAN PARTICIPATION AND OPPORTUNITY

In the US the emphasis on fraud in the context of welfare has far outstripped emphasis on fraud in income tax evasion. For example, television adverts and newspapers circulated telephone numbers exclusively for reporting welfare fraud during 1996 and 1997. The concern in this context is that the media emphasis on fraud amongst welfare recipients rather than the whole population connects poverty with dishonesty in the public image. For parents with children enduring a crisis in income maintenance, it is an added burden to link welfare so clearly with fraud and also perpetuates the idea that welfare is something to be ashamed of and a drain on the economy.

The support of families with young children to enable them to raise their children and to thrive through income maintenance, education and training, costs the taxpayer much less than the state support of a child removed from home for reasons of child protection or neglect. As revealed by Courtney, one of the dangers of the current minimal and time limited welfare programs in the US, is the resulting strain on family relationships and the increasing incidence of child abuse: 'The incidence of abuse and neglect is approximately 22 times higher among families with incomes below $15,000 per year than among families with incomes of more than $30,000 per year.'[30] In this research the key variable leading to abuse is poverty; similarly in the profiles of residential homes and foster parenting, the key characteristic of the children receiving these services is poverty.

Fraud is reprehensible; however, it is unhelpful and undermining of the well-being of families to use the actions of a small percentage of welfare recipients to define the majority. Unfortunately those policy makers who prefer limited government involvement in relation to poverty find it advantageous to label welfare recipients as criminal or fraudulent, even though we know that the overwhelming majority of those recipients are young children. To label someone in poverty as deviant is to distance them from 'people like us' and reduces the responsibility of society as a whole. This discussion takes us into questions of morality, our fourth and final layer of concern.

CONTINUING TO DEFINE WELFARE AS A QUESTION OF MORALITY RATHER THAN SOCIAL OBLIGATION

The emphasis of policy makers on morality as connected to poverty is self-righteous and politically volatile. Although Lord Harris bemoans the loss of a generation who knew thrift and hard work, we know that, then and now, the burden of poverty is carried by children. US media emphasize the dependency and implied choice of people to be 'on' welfare with derogatory references to 'welfare moms'. However, rather than being dependent drains on society, recipients are often raising children on budgets that require extreme dexterity to survive: in Minnesota $532 (approximately £355) per month for a mother and

FIGURE 5.3: **Spectrum of welfare policy issues: three interacting systems**

	POLITICAL	**SOCIAL**	**ECONOMIC**
1. STRUCTURAL			
Recommendations	• universal child benefit • access to higher education • review of occupational welfare to middle class women • persuade voters solutions to poverty belong to us all	• inclusion of people in poverty in planning • invoke choice • educate about the income gap	• offer tax incentives to employers • balance public/ corporate welfare • universal child benefit/tax credit • attention to re-distribution of wealth
Barriers	• some are undeserving	• lack of perception of common good	• emphasis on tax reduction
2. COMMUNITY			
Recommendations	• efficient transport • child care facilities expanded • public/private partnerships • affordable housing • teenage pregnancy prevention	• carpooling and network of support • family friendly employers • public education about poverty • home share • listen to people's stories • mentoring programmes	• neighbourhood included in administering grants • local tax incentives to employers for re-training • expand Habitat for Humanity
Barriers	• stigma & group labelling	• rural isolation	• lack of investment in low income areas
3. INDIVIDUAL			
Recommendations	• become politically active • learn about resources • vote for re-training & educational schemes	• network with people concerned about child poverty	• lobby for choice, eg employ child care or stay at home & receive income support
Barriers	• gender discrimination in valuing home-making as work • lack of well-paid part-time work	• isolation • loss of self-esteem	

child barely covers rent and heat let alone all the costs of clothes, transport and school, and in most states the grant is much less.

As discussed earlier in this book, in Britain in the 1890s it was popular to judge those in poverty as slothful and without moral fibre. A turning point was Lloyd George's 'war budget' speech of 1911 which presented issues of poverty as challenging to us all. Since then outdated and judgmental attitudes have re-emerged amongst those who have never had to seek an unemployment or income maintenance cheque and indeed often inherit or gain wealth without their own direct labour. Thus, we have the irony in the US of a country which has the richest people in the world, the 'spectacularly rich', moving with insufficient concern amongst the poorest, who are often children. The President in introducing the new legislation referred to the 'moral obligation to help poor people help themselves.' However, there is a wage structure in place in the US which sustains the wealth of the few and makes it very difficult for poor families to escape their plight.

Nearly half of Head Start (a federally funded pre-school preparation programme) parents are working and approximately 40 per cent of people receiving energy assistance work, yet are still poor. Poverty is defined by income. By this measure a family of three with less than $12,980 (£8,655) in annual income (1997 figures) is officially in poverty. More than 30 million Americans are officially in poverty.[31]

Welfare reform could be about policies which secure the future of children by helping to maintain stable, well employed and educated households. However, while the emphasis is on morality rather than social obligation, the focus on children's well-being will continue to be obscured at great future cost.

SUMMARY AND AVENUES FOR THE FUTURE

Recommendations for the future will address the following areas of poverty: structural, community and individual. Figure 5.3 (page 00) sets out the levels of possible intervention and outlines possible policies and actions.

STRUCTURAL ELEMENTS OF POVERTY

When referring to the 'structural' elements of recommendations for welfare reform, we mean the largest units of organization in our national (and international) systems and the way these larger units affect individual lives collectively and beyond the control of the individual. For example, when a large plant closes in Sheffield or Swansea, the decisions have been taken following corporate assessment of collective loss of market and revenue; the individual who supplies the lunch counter or the shop floor employee who is laid off had no direct role in this decision and cannot therefore be 'blamed' for his or her lack of work. Structural changes make an impact on the whole community for good or ill. When policy makers have a structural approach to welfare reform, they recognize that the infrastructure of access to and definition of work, child care, transport, education is a prerequisite to hasty pressures at the individual level and their goals are to:

- Reframe the concept of 'welfare recipients' to people just like us and most often children, who need government intervention to balance the vagaries of the marketplace.
- Re-classify who works in the home in order to avoid the paradox of childcare workers being included in the workforce while parents are excluded.
- Make child care benefits through children's allowances or earned income integrated tax credit universal and *adequate*.
- Cut the stigma. Include all members of the neighbourhood as part of the fabric of society where all are involved in solutions to poverty.

COMMUNITY ELEMENTS OF POVERTY

When referring to the community role in reforming welfare, the Blair government has achieved an expansion of investment in local programmes, such as the breakfast clubs and family literacy projects discussed in Chapter 4. While the UK may have copied exemplars of current US partnerships and raised the expectation that corporate officials work together with the towns and villages where they reside, the current results, for example in terms of 'family friendly' employers, are marginal. A national community focus includes projects that mentor children in poverty; it looks to the well-being and neighbourliness of people and invokes a sense of social responsibility rather than blaming and making accusations of dependency. The following goals and recommendations for welfare reform at the community level can be made.

- Raise tax incentives to employers who offer varieties of training, child-care, recruitment and retention supports for people re-entering or joining the workforce.
- Gather the successes of communities, corporations and other countries into public education videos, messages and public meetings.
- Assume people in poverty have strengths and resilience that are untapped while they are excluded from mainstream life and make this a clear public message.
- Include people experiencing poverty as participants in planning and implementing change.

MICRO INDIVIDUAL ELEMENTS OF POVERTY

Historically the emphasis in the US has always been at the individual level in regard to welfare reform. Adults and children have been labelled as dependent and unwilling to work. The solution is therefore easy for the rest of us: if you are to blame for being unemployed, just get back to work. However, our analysis and current reports sounding warnings in the US about the consequences of welfare reform for children, reveal the complex layers of contributing factors at both individual and community levels. A powerful way to turn the tide, from traditional approaches to welfare reform, to a more effective future in terms of the well-being of children, is to take up the challenge of truly knowing what the experience of poverty means to those enduring it, particularly the 'quiet problems' of hungry and homeless children.

Goals for policy makers (readers, all of us) for a re-framed approach to the individual level of welfare reform would therefore include the following:

- Live the experience of poverty, even the smallest time. Visit and talk with people using Family Centre services in impoverished areas or shelters or drop in centres for those on the streets. It is crucial for policy makers to know the benefit of personal contact, interest and recognition.
- Support investment in programmes of 'Life Long Learning' and 'Early Excellence Centres.'
- Give children alternatives to lives of poverty.

In Salter's article, 'When Want becomes Greed...', the question is posed...when will we be ready to call a halt to the patterns of child poverty and engage in recognition of social obligation and the sharing of well-being? The current platform of the Labour Party suggests that we are slowly beginning to engage in that recognition, but this book cautions against any idea that US welfare reform has been good to children in the poorest families.

SUMMARY OF QUESTIONS POSED IN CHAPTER 1

HOW DOES THE US WELFARE REFORM STAND AS AN ANTI-POVERTY STRATEGY?

The Personal Responsibility and Work Opportunity Reconciliation Act is being implemented in ways that narrowly construe the intent of the legislation as being to reduce dependency and get recipients to work. The legislation may have achieved reductions in the numbers of people applying for and receiving income maintenance in several states including Wisconsin, Georgia, Florida; it cannot, however, be claimed to be either reforming or anti-poverty while the numbers of children in poverty continue to grow. The Children's Defense Fund 1998 report, *After Welfare, Many Families Fare Worse*, based on figures from over 30 state and local studies, states that:

> Of the former welfare recipients who find work, 71 per cent earn less than $250 per week, less than the poverty level for a family of three… We must face the fact that families with extremely low wages do not earn enough to raise their children out of poverty. Without help like child care, transportation, training and wage supplements, families are one crisis away from joblessness or hunger… In many cities, easily one in 10 families in homeless shelters say they are there because of welfare cuts.[32]

Now the spring 2000 Berkeley/Yale study of 948 single mothers with children finds that there is a 'migration of children into mediocre child care' although we know that 'the education of the adult the child spends his or her day with is one of the strongest predictors of child development.'[33]

WHAT ARE THE IMPLICATIONS OF 'WELFARE REFORM' FOR CHILDREN IN POOR FAMILIES?

The focus has been on adults and work in ways that discounted dialogue concerned with the long-term benefits or problems for children. In research on the impact of welfare reform on migrant farm workers, Rosenthal writes:

> Last fall migrant children returned to school hungrier, more ill-clothed, and in worse health than ever before. While these children generally have been considered at risk, their fragile lives are under the greatest stress in decades. Welfare reform clearly is taking its toll on migrant families in significant ways, with particular impact on migrant children.[34]

Interim reports from California, Wisconsin and Georgia speak of success in terms of moving parents, usually lone mothers, back into the workforce, but the constant caution is that the majority are entering low paid work with high turnover and minimal qualifications and that children are faring worse rather than better as a result of this legislation. We say yes to work that retrains, offers a living wage and family-friendly policies; no to work at any cost, especially if that cost is the well-being of children.

WHICH PARTS OF THE 'REFORM' ARE MOST EFFECTIVE

There is no doubt that the most eye catching elements of the reform are the work partnerships between employers and public agencies. Within these partnerships we see employers such as Xerox Business Systems reviewing their retention policies and considering the special needs of people involved in the transition from welfare to work. Government incentives to employers to re-train, offer bridging programs and co-operate with public job placement agencies for people re-entering the workforce are among the more promising and politically viable possibilities for welfare reform legislation. The renewed concern for family-friendly workplaces represents a shift in attention to the expanding female workforce and the attendant needs of children and elder care. Similarly, housing and transport are being recognized as major barriers to employment, and this is leading to new joint ventures between non-profit and private sector organizations which represent innovative programs to support families with children in achieving viable, above minimum income. This is a crucial area for growth in the UK and one which, as demonstrated in Chapter 4, is receiving uneven and inadequate attention from the Government.

IS THE EMPHASIS ON EMPLOYMENT AT ALL COSTS FEASIBLE?

It is a paradox that US states such as California, Minnesota, Wisconsin, are experiencing a period of labour shortage even while the income gap continues to grow between the affluent and the poor. In the Citizen's League report, *A Labor Shortage and a Leadership Challenge*, State economists and demographers are raising issues of an ageing workforce, the uneven location of workers between urban and rural areas, the cost of housing preventing mobility and the question of education and preparation of workers. The shortage of labour is discussed as an opportunity rather than a problem, an opportunity which if tackled in a collaborative way can have 'a significant impact on the long-term well-being of Minnesota…this isn't about averting a disaster. Rather, it's about lifting the expected standard of living beyond that which would otherwise have been attained.'[35] Unfortunately, without parallel recognition of the needs of welfare recipients with low educational qualifications, very young children, inexperience and restricted mobility (transport, housing location, child care etc), it is unlikely that the lifting of the standard of living for some Americans will benefit children in poverty.

The State of Minnesota is seen as leading the way in responding to labour needs and is therefore an important harbinger of the ways other states will respond to changing demographics. The key question remains: can the opportunity of labour shortages be turned to the advantage of people experiencing poverty? The Citizens League asks whether these changes will simply mean continued success for some and exclusion for others or whether the focus will be on redistribution.

> There is great hope that we will be able to hire people that have previously been on welfare, that have had very little job training or job experience, that they'll now have all sorts of opportunities open up. In fact, this does seem to be happening, because welfare rolls have been sharply downward for about the last four years. Issues like transportation, job-skill training, child care still need to be resolved.[36]

It remains a frustrating puzzle specialists and state economists are so ready to interpret the reduction in welfare rolls as evidence that people in poverty are succeeding in the workplace. Certainly some are, but we also know from the Department of Human Services and employment counsellors that many families are being sanctioned for failure to comply with workfare regulations and that these families simply drop from sight when they fail to meet job requirements. As others enter the workforce their children enter a variety of care settings. In the Berkeley/Yale studies of mothers in Connecticut, Florida and California, two thirds of their children entered child care centres, while one third were cared for by family, neighbours, or friends. The study co-director, Fuller, reports that: 'In the centres, 65 per cent of the teachers or caregivers had some training beyond high school, while in the homes only 39 per cent had higher education.'[37]

IS THE CHANGE FROM WELFARE TO WORK MORE FOR POLITICAL EFFECT THAN RAISING PEOPLE OUT OF POVERTY?

Certainly for Edelman, in his article 'The Worst thing Bill Clinton has done', there is no doubt that the central goal of welfare reform is budget reduction. Budget reduction, devolution of power to individual states through block grants and a period of popularity for reducing central government, all confirm that the political gains are greater than the gains for children's well-being. The goal of reforming an outdated system is generally welcomed and has resulted in some of the benefits addressed here. However, there can be little doubt that scant attention was given to the more complex and long-term goals of reducing the poverty of children. The irony remains that, if work is considered the only solution, then children suffer and costs for children's services increase.

SHOULD THIS APPROACH TO 'WELFARE REFORM' BE TRANSPLANTED TO THE UK?

This book has identified some of the central issues concerning families in poverty in the US and their interaction with welfare reform. Our research has shown that Thatcher's admiration of the US has carried into the Blair administration. The focus in the UK on the language of welfare reform and 'job seeking,' the emphasis on value laden issues such as 'dependency' and 'new deals' are direct reflections of US policy. Furthermore, while the UK has articulated a commitment to ending poverty for children, it is clearly not the expectation currently in the US. The focus on 'back to work', and the sanctions which first reduce and then drop people from rolls, illustrate short-term policy, not intended as anti-poverty but focused on cost reduction and the marketplace. The US 'War on Poverty' of the 1960s identified the many complex layers relating to poverty and implemented preventive programmes, such as Head Start early education services and public health education, plus health services and immunization clinics. Issues of poverty were not isolated to an excluded and stigmatized few. However, the innovation of the 1960s did not last for complex reasons, including the changes in economic capacity, the distractions of the Vietnam War and the increasing power of the conservative economic voices who wanted limited government intervention.

The strategies within US style welfare reform that can be seen to have the most impact are those engaging people to seek employment and which connect back to the marketplace. However, the consequences of US welfare reform also include an increase in people without income supports. The United Nations Declaration on the Rights of the Child asserts the right of every child to food, clothing, shelter, a name. The current focus of US welfare reform may never have been intended as an anti-poverty strategy, but the criminalizing approach used in terms of sanctions and cut-offs shows little regard to the basic needs of children.

There is a chart topping rap tune called 'I will buy you a garden where flowers will grow'. The lyrics object to the popular notion that money can't buy you happiness, that's the story of 'you who never knew the joy of a welfare Christmas'. For most people, the hardships for children when parents are trying to manage birthdays, celebrations, holidays on a minimum budget, cannot be imagined. In a culture which judges by external assets, when you are what you have, it is politically elusive to engage support for directing resources to the 'have nots'.

Poverty is a crisis for any of us experiencing it. To survive with young children on a minimum wage takes all the initiative and creativity possible – why is it so hard to believe that? Perhaps the business plan of the UK Midland Bank is a case in point. The 'family friendly' policies came about because the Bank discovered that they were losing money by training people who would then leave to have families. It takes a year's salary to replace and train a new person. For every community in Britain and the US, ever increasing tax monies are needed to maintain human services for families in crisis, children's homes, prisons, correctional systems. Re-directed resources to the needs of children so that they can grow and thrive within their families, can combat those expenditures – but it takes vision, backing away from hasty solutions and willingness to address at least some of the ten recommendations made here.

In Chapter 4, Karen Lyons quoted a UK Government Green Paper[38] as identifying the following four stages of welfare:

1. Stopping outright destitution.
2. Alleviating poverty.
3. Preventing poverty.
4. Promoting opportunity and developing potential.

Currently in the US, the sanctions and concept of 'cut-off' create destitution for the children of the families concerned. If the UK continues to adopt (by terminology and posture) US style welfare reform there is no doubt that it will be turning back from its claims to be in stage 3: prevention of poverty. The US Welfare Reform has been a disaster for children and families who remain below the minimum wage or who face sanctions (often without understanding why). Quite simply, despite some learning from the legislative process, the US policy as it stands is wrong for the UK because of:

- its emphasis on work at any price;
- its use of sanctions and punishments for people who fail to comply;
- its lack of attention to the consequences for children in families without income;
- its lack of provision when 2002 turns and families are 'cut-off;'
- the political ploy of caricaturing people experiencing poverty as different, dependent and a drain; and
- the removal of dignity for lone parents with young children.

US style welfare reform will not help to halve the number of children in poverty in the next ten years in the UK. The US experiment can, however, give UK policy-makers some lessons and some insights on areas for change especially in the area of public-private collaboration. However, the confusion and stigma that have resulted from misuse of the term 'welfare' suggests that we have dire need of fresh words and meaning. The UK should reject US terminology and re-claim the tradition of concern for those in poverty, by building policies which use the language of well-being, open gateway, inclusion and dignity.

RECOMMENDATIONS TO GUIDE UK
WELFARE REFORM

1. Reframe the concept of 'welfare recipients' to people just like us and most often children, who need government intervention to balance the vagaries of the marketplace. Avoid US terminology of dependents and sanctions.

2. Re-classify who works in the home to end the paradox of childcare workers in homes being included in the workforce while lone parents in poverty are excluded.

3. Make child care benefits through increased children's allowances or integrated child credit universal and adequate (in line with raising children's families above the poverty line). US policy has been successful in reducing 'welfare rolls' and unsuccessful in reducing the numbers of children in poverty.

4. Cut the stigma. Include all members of the neighbourhood as part of the fabric of society where all are involved in solutions to poverty. Avoid the contradiction of US policy stigmatizing the poor for parenting in the home while supporting the wealthy homemaker through tax breaks for employed spouse.

5. Raise tax incentives to employers who offer varieties of training, child-care, recruitment and retention of people re-entering or joining the workforce.

6. Gather the successes of communities, corporations and other countries into public education videos, messages and town meetings.

7. Assume people in poverty have strengths and resilience that are untapped while they are excluded from mainstream life. Demonstrate this assumption with policies which raise the minimum wage with respectful use of language in policy materials, press releases and public discourse and by including people experiencing poverty as participants in planning.

8. Live the experience of poverty, even the smallest time. Visit and talk with people using Family Centre services in impoverished areas or shelters or drop in centres for those on the streets.

9. Support nation wide investment in programs of 'Life Long Learning' and 'Centres of Excellence.'

10. Give children alternatives to lives of poverty and listen to their stories and voices.

NOTES

1 N Theodore & J Peck, Welfare to Work: National Problems, Local Solutions? *Critical Social Policy*, 1999.

2 M Kramer, *Cornerstone*, quoted in 'How Welfare-to-Work is Working: Welfare Reform through the eyes of Minnesota employers, welfare participants and local partnerships', McKnight Foundation and Wilder Research Center, 2000, p7.

3 L McNichol, *Pulling Apart: State Income Inequalities*, Center on Budget and Policy Priorities, CBPP, 1997. www.cbpp.org/pa/rel/htm

4 J Rogaly, *Financial Times*, 31 July 1999.

5 J Hopfensperger, 'Study assesses who's succeeding under welfare rules', *Star Tribune*, March 22nd, 2000.

6 E Annie, *Kids Count*, Casey Foundation, 1999.

7 L Engelhardt, *Bread for the World*, BFTW, 1998.

8 M J Bane & R Weissbourd, 'Welfare Reform and Children', *Stanford Law and Policy Review*, vol. 9:1, 1998.

9 C Germain, *Human Behavior in the Social Environment*, Columbia, 1994.

10 K Seccombe, 'So you think I drive a cadillac?' *Welfare Recipients' Perspectives on the System and its Reform*, Allyn & Bacon, 1999.

11 A Faber & E Mazlish, *How to Talk so Kids will Listen & Listen so Kids will talk*, Avon, 1982.

12 G Goleman, *Emotional Intelligence*, 1997.

13 Editorial, 'Welfare reserves don't transfer money out of the system', *Star Tribune*, 10 February 1999.

14 P Hewitt, 'How We Will Build a New Jerusalem', *The Times*, 26 March 1998.

15 R Harris, 'Betrayal of a Generation', *The Times*, 26 March, 1998.

16 S Mark Broin, VP Information Services, International Dairy Queen Inc., *Star Tribune*, 13 June 1998.

17 www2.state.ga.us/BROC/peach.html

18 S Ohlemacher, *Welfare Reform Lagging*, 2000. www.lexis-nexis.com/universe/doc

19 Bane & Weissbourd, (note 7).

20 Social Services Parliamentary Monitor 'New Deal for Lone Parents: Recipients praise its success in talks with Ministers', Issue No. 037, 24 January 2000.

21 B Rushe, 'Welfare Sanctions would get tougher under bill, Joint Religious Legislative Coalition', *Star Tribune*, 25 February 2000.

22 J J Wilson, *When Work Disappears*, Vintage, 1998.

23 J Pawasarat & F Stetzer, *Removing Transportation Barriers to Employment: Assessing Driver's License and Vehicle Ownership Patterns of Low-Income Populations*, University of Wisconsin-Milwaukee Employment and Training Institute, July 1998 & www.uwm.edu/Dept/ETI/dot.html

24 Wilder Research Center 'How Welfare-to-Work is Working', McNight Foundation, 2000.

25 Moser Report, *A Fresh Start: Basic Skills for Adults*, DfEE, 1999.

26 B Fuller & S Kagan, *Remember the Children: Mothers Balance Work and Child Care under Welfare Reform*, Graduate School of Education-PACE University of California, Berkeley 94720, 2000.

27 John Pawasarat & Lois Quinn, *Removing Barriers to Employment: The Child Care-Jobs Equation*, University of Wisconsin-Milwaukee Employment and Training Institute, 1998.

28 Childrens' Defense Fund, 1997

29 R Lister, *Citizenship: Feminist Perspectives*, Macmillan, 1997.

30 Mark Courtney, 'The Costs of Child Protection in the Context of Welfare Reform', *Protecting Children From Abuse and Neglect*, Vol. 8 No. 1, Spring 1998.

31 D DeVaan, 'Reforms to end poverty', *Minneapolis Star Tribune*, 4 January 1997.

32 www.childrensdefense.org/release 9812o2.html

33 Fuller & Kagan, (note 26).

34 R Rosenthal, The Impact of Welfare Reform on Migrant Farm worker Families, *Clearinghouse Review*, Jan–Feb, 1998.

35 Citizens League Minnesota, *A labor shortage and a leadership challenge*, 1998. www.citizensleague.net

36 Citizens League, (note 35).

37 Fuller & Kagan, (note 26).

38 Welfare Reform Focus Files, HMSO, March 1998

APPENDIX 1

THE PHILADELPHIA INQUIRER

MARCH 3, 1999
CITY OF PHILADELPHIA OFFICE OF THE MAYOR

Dear Greater Philadelphia Residents:

We will face a welfare crisis – sooner or later.

A growing number of voices are saying that Philadelphia is not due for a welfare reform crisis. Let me dissuade you of this myth. Literally thousands of mothers and children are likely to become penniless this spring and summer after the state's two-year time limit on welfare benefits kicks in.

The naysayers point to our regional economy, which is flush with jobs, as a sign that we face no welfare reform crisis. Currently, this is true: about 8,000 entry-level jobs are expected to be available to those leaving welfare over the next year in the Philadelphia area. We intend to fill every one of those jobs with welfare recipients through Greater Philadelphia Work, the City's ambitious welfare-to-work program.

But with more than 36,000 Philadelphia households slated to be kicked off welfare by September, 8,000 jobs isn't going to be enough.

To see what happens when there aren't enough jobs for welfare recipients, we need only look to a state that is a favorite of the welfare-reform optimists: Wisconsin. In a recent study, 62 per cent of those leaving welfare in Wisconsin were employed when interviewed six months after they had left the rolls. Wisconsin's program has been hailed as a tremendous success, and no other state has even come close in matching this rate of success in employing former welfare recipients.

But remember, a 62 per cent success rate means a 38 per cent failure rate. More than a third of those leaving welfare in Wisconsin lost their benefits without finding a job. This failure rate has caused a host of additional problems; for example, a full third of all families interviewed said that there had been times when they could not afford to buy food.

Even if Philadelphia performs as well in employing welfare recipients as the most successful state in the nation, we can still expect at least 38 per cent of those hitting the deadline to lose their benefits without finding a job. In Philadelphia, 38 per cent represents about 14,000 families who will be thrown off the welfare rolls by September without finding a job – a total of nearly 40,000 mothers and their children.

As these families fight to survive, they will seek the City's help to obtain even the most basic necessities:

– HOUSING. Only a small proportion of the welfare caseload resides in public housing. Most welfare recipients need their welfare checks in order to meet the rent. If just half of the 40,000 people losing benefits without jobs are evicted and unable to find alternate housing, the City's homeless services system will be flooded with 20,000 additional people – which would quadruple the number of homeless individuals we currently serve on a daily basis. The average family stays in shelter for about five months. Cost to the City: $36 million.

– FOSTER CARE. The destitution caused by welfare reform will sadly make it impossible for some families to care for their children, forcing these children into foster care. In Wisconsin, five per cent of those leaving welfare said they had been forced to abandon their children. If just five per cent of the 26,000 children losing welfare benefits in Philadelphia end up in foster care, the City's already overwhelmed Department of Human Services will need to find placements for 1,300 kids. Funded by a mixture of federal, state and City dollars, these placements cost three times more than if the children's parents were simply permitted to keep their welfare grants. Cost to the City: about $1 million per year, and another $7.5 million in federal and state dollars.

– HEALTH CARE. Although most people who lose their welfare checks can continue to get Medical Assistance, many are cut off from medical benefits inadvertently. These families turn to the City's health centers for care. It is not unreasonable to expect each of the 40,000 people to visit a health center at least once each year. Cost to the City: $4.6 million.

– TRANSPORTATION TO SCHOOL. Using estimates derived from the number of children who travel to school on SEPTA, we expect that more than 3,800 children from families losing their welfare benefits may have no way to pay for the transit fare they need to get to school. The burden of these costs could fall on the City. Cost: $1.2 million per year.

As these scenarios demonstrate, welfare reform is not just a crisis affecting thousands of individuals; it also has the potential to offset many of the City's hard-won fiscal accomplishments over the last seven years. The total annual costs potentially faced by the City due to welfare reform – $42.8 million – is larger than the budgets of many City departments, including Streets, Recreation, and the Free Library.

To avoid this human and fiscal catastrophe, I continue to call for changes in state law that can make welfare reform more humane for welfare mothers and their children, and decrease the likelihood that they will flood the City's social services system for help. These changes include:

- End the policy of cutting welfare benefits to the entire family – rather than only the head of the household – when a welfare mother fails to comply with work requirements. Pennsylvania is only of only 14 states with this overly harsh rule.
- Join the 31 states nationwide that permit welfare recipients to count training and education toward their required hours of work, rather than forcing women to quit school to fulfill their work requirements at a dead-end job.
- Take the hundreds of millions of dollars in savings accumulated by the state due to welfare reform and spend it on creating improved child care, transportation, and training opportunities for those on the welfare rolls.

The bottom line is that even in the best of cases, tens of thousands of Philadelphians could be thrown off the welfare rolls come September with no jobs. Unless substantial changes are made to our state's welfare laws, we will indeed face a welfare reform crisis – either sooner or later.

Sincerely yours,

Edward G. Rendell
Mayor.

APPENDIX 2

USEFUL LINKS

http://newfederalism.urban.org
'Assessing the New Federalism is a multi-year Urban Institute research project to analyse the devolution of responsibility for social programs from the federal government to the states, focussing primarily on health care, income security, job training, and social services.'
(Link to Child Welfare and you will find many articles about different issues in child welfare).

http://www.statepolicy.org/html/welref.htm
Influencing State Policy: Welfare Reform Resources
Report, News, Resources and other Links

http://www.childrensdefense.org/
There are many facts, figures and reports on America's child welfare. See report 'From Welfare to What?'

http://cpmcnet.columbia.edu/dept/nccp
National Center for Children in Poverty
Links to news, media resources, newsletters, child poverty facts, information, research and publications.
http://cpmcnet.columbia.edu/dept/nccp/main8.html contains articles published on Children and Welfare reform. Statistics, facts sheets, and other information on Child Poverty.

http://www.unicef.org
United Nation's Children Fund
Information on Child Rights, news and statistics.

http://www.undp.org/
United Nations Development Programme
Focus areas in Poverty, Gender, Environment, and Governance containing information, news and statistics.

http://www.epn.org/ideacentral/welfare
The Electronic Policy Network
Access to articles on healthcare, unemployment, poverty, wages, and leave. Also see, **http://www.epn.org/links/welfarelinks.html** for

Welfare Reform: The National Debate and State and Local welfare reform. Get a background on poverty and welfare reform and read about government position on welfare reform.

http://www.welfaretowork.org/wtwpapps/wtwphome.nsf
This is a web-site about an organization called: The Welfare to Work Partnership. This organization helps business hire welfare recipients.

http://www.acf.dhhs.gov/news/welfare/index.htm
Contains guidance and status documents, links and research materials, statistics, MOE and allocation tables, and more.

http://www.now.org/issues/economic/welfref.html
An article called, Action Alert on Welfare Reform, July 9th, 1996. There's a link to NOW (National Organization for Women) and Welfare and it gives a list of NOW actions and issue info.

http://www.lincproject.org
Links to low-income organizing efforts, news, and organizer's online toolkit. And an article link to TANF Reauthorization.

http://www.calib.com/nccanch
National Clearinghouse on Child Abuse and Neglect Info resource for professionals seeking info on the prevention, identification, and treatment of child abuse and welfare issues.

http://www.cwla.org/
Child Welfare League of America – Links to advocacy, programs, publication, conferences and training, consultation and member agencies.

http://www.basw.co.uk/
British Association of Social Workers. Links to job vacancies, Branch News, publications, press releases, policy responses, web-site content upholds the BASW code of ethics for social work.

http://www.cswe.org
Links to social work associations and annual conferences of social educators and researchers.

http://www.socialworkers.org/
Links about NASW, publications, services, resources, news and info.

http://www.uiowa.edu/~nrcfcp
Links to an overview and service and resources. National Resource Centre for Family Centered Practice. Children's permanence, state and federal policy, effective program models, successful intervention strategies, and strengthening families.

http://www.tmn.com/
'We help groups and organizations build teams and learning communities through our organization development consulting, web-based conferencing, and facilitation services.'

http://www.childrennow.org/
Children Now utilizes research and mass communications to make the well being of children a top priority across the nation.

http://www.cyfc.umn.edu
Web-site for the children, youth and family consortium with information and resources on children's well-being.

http://socwork.uindy.edu/links/search1.htm
Search Tools for Social Work – Search engine with different kinds of search options for social work.

http://www.co.hennepin.mn.us/commhlth/reports/shape.htm
Survey of the Health of Adults, the Population and the Environment. This is used to assess the health status of residents in Hennepin County, Minnesota. Contains links to reports, city and state resources, and web-sites pertaining to all kinds of areas of 'health' and effects of welfare reform.

http://www.americaradioworks.org
A report on child poverty in the US. 'The Forgotten 14 million.'

http://www.womensenews.org
Women's E-News. Links to woman issues. Links to an article about the decline in health coverage of women leaving welfare.

http://www.wilder.org/wrc
Links to research on welfare to works, poverty, families, and communities.

http://www.mcknight.org
Web-site about the McKnight Foundation including their mission, goals, services and news in the community. (See report 'How Welfare to Work is Working')

http://www.welfareinfo.org
Links to program and management related resources, topics, welfare related events, and human service tools. Also links to Federal and State plans. Includes research, references and data resources.

http://www.bc.edu/bc_org/avp/gssw/social_welfare_policy.htm
Link to the Journal of Social Policy.

http://www.nyu.edu/socialwork.wwwrsw/
Links by government, reference, journals and newsletters, social work. higher education and search and general indexes.

http://ssw.che.umn.edu/cascw/
Winter 2000 practice notes, background and mission, and recent publications links. Also, links to the University of Minnesota.

APPENDIX 3

UN CONVENTION ON THE RIGHTS OF THE CHILD

SUMMARY OF SUBSTANTIVE ARTICLES

Article 1
Definition of Child
Every person under 18, unless national law grants majority at an earlier age.

Article 2
Freedom from Discrimination
Rights in the Convention apply to ill children without exception; the State to protect children from any form of discrimination or punishment based on Family's status, activities or beliefs.

Article 3
Best Interest of a Child
The best interests of the child to prevail in all legal and administrative decisions; the State to ensure the establishment of institutional standards for the care and protection of children.

Article 4
Implementation of Rights
The State to translate the rights in this Convention into actually.

Article 5
Respect for Parental responsibility
The State to respect the rights of parents or guardians to provide direction to the child in the exercise of the rights in this Convention.

Article 6
Survivals & Development
The child's right to life; the State to ensure the survival and maximum development of the child.

Article 7
Name & Nationality
The right to a name and to acquire a nationality, the right to know and be cared for by parents.

Article 8
Preservation of Identity
The right to preserve or re-establish the child's identity (name, nationality, and family ties).

Article 9
Parental Care & Non-Separation
The right to live with parents unless this is deemed incompatible with the child's best interests; the right to maintain contact with both parents; the State to provide information when separation results from State action.

Article 10
Family Reunification
The right to leave or enter any country for family reunification and to maintain contact with both parents.

Article 11
Illicit Transfer and Non-Return
The State to combat the illicit transfer and non-return of children.

Article 12
Free Expression of Opinion
The child's right to express an opinion in matters affecting the child and to have that opinion heard.

Article 13
Freedom of Information
The right to seek, receive, and impart information through any media.

Article 14
Freedom of Thought, Conscience, & Religion
The right to determine and practise any belief, State to respect the rights of parents or guardians to provide direction in the exercise of this right.

Article 15
Freedom of Association
The right to freedom of association and freedom of peaceful assembly.

Article 16
Protection of Privacy
The right to protection from arbitrary or unlawful interference with privacy, family, home, or correspondence, or attacks on honor and reputation.

Article 17
Media & Information
The State to ensure access to information and material from a diversity of national and international sources.

Article 18
Parental Responsibilities
The State to recognize the principle that both parents are responsible for the upbringing of their children and that parents or guardians have primary responsibility, the State to assist parents or guardians in this responsibility and ensure the provision of child care for eligible working parents.

Article 19
Abuse & Neglect
The State to protect children from all forms of abuse, neglect, and exploitation by parents or others, and to undertake preventive and treatment programs in this regard.

Article 20
Children without Families
The right to receive special protection and assistance from the State when deprived of family environment and to be provided with alternative care, such as foster placement or Kafala of Islamic law, adoption, or institutional placement.

Article 21
Adoption
The State to regulate the process of adoption (including intercountry adoption), where it is permitted.

Article 22
Refugee Children
The State to ensure protection and assistance to children who are refugees or are seeking refugee status, and to cooperate with competent organizations providing such protection and assistance.

Article 23
Disabled Children
The right of disabled children to special care and training designed to help achieve self-reliance and a full and decent life in society.

Article 24
Health Care
the right to the highest attainable standard of health and access to medical services; the State to attempt to diminish infant and child mortality, combat disease, and malnutrician, ensure health care for expectant mothers, provide access to health education, develop preventive health care, and abolish harmful traditional practices.

Article 25
Periodic Review
The right of children placed by the State for reasons of care, protection, or treatment to have all aspects of that placement reviewed regularly.

Article 26
Social Security
The right, where appropriate, to benefit from social security or insurance.

Article 27
Standard of Living
The right to an adequate standard of living; the State to assist parents who cannot meet this responsibility and to try to recover maintenance for the child from persons having financial responsibility, both within the State and abroad.

Article 28
Education
The right to education; the State to provide free and compulsory primary education, ensure equal access to secondary and higher education, and ensure that school discipline does not threaten the child's human dignity.

Article 29
Aims of Education
The States Parties' agreement that education be directed at developing the child's personality and talents; to prepare the child for responsible life in a free society, develop respect for the child's parents, basic human rights, the natural environment, and the child's own cultural and national values and those of others.

Article 30
Children of Minorities
The right of children of minority communities and indigenous populations to enjoy their own culture, practice their own religion, and use their own language.

Article 31
Leisure & Recreation
The right to leisure, play, and participation in cultural and artistic activities.

Article 32
Child Labor
The right to be protected from economic exploitation and from engaging in work that constitutes a threat to health, education, and development; the State to set minimum ages for employment, regulate conditions of employment, and provide sanctions for effective enforcement.

Article 33
Narcotics
The State to protect children from illegal narcotic and psychotropic drugs and from involvement in their production or distribution.

Article 34
Sexual Exploitation
The State to protect children from sexual exploitation and abuse, including prostitution and involvement in pornography.

Article 35
Sale & Trafficking
The State to prevent the abduction, sale, and trafficking of children.

Article 36
Other Exploitation
The State to protect children from all other forms of exploitation.

Article 37
Torture, Capital Punishment, and Deprivation of Liberty
The State to protect children from torture or other cruel, inhuman, or degrading treatment; capital punishment or life imprisonment for offences committed by persons below the age of 18; and unlawful or arbitrary deprivation of liberty. The right of children deprived of liberty to be treated with humanity and respect, to be separated from adults, to maintain contact with family member, and to have prompt access to legal assistance.

Article 38
Armed Conflict
The State to respect international humanitarian law, ensure that no child under 15 takes a direct part in hostilities, refrain from recruiting any child under 15 into the armed forces, and ensure that all children affected by armed conflict benefit from protection and care.

Article 39
Rehabilitative Care
The State to promote the physical and psychological recovery and social reintegration of child victims of abuse, neglect, exploitation, torture, or armed conflicts in an environment which fosters the health, self-respect and dignity of the child.

Article 40
Juvenile Justice
The right of accused children to be treated with dignity. The State to ensure that: no child is accused by reason of acts or omissions not prohibited by law at the time committed; every accused child is informed promptly of the charges, presumed innocent until proven guilty in a prompt and fair trial, receives legal assistance and is not compelled to give testimony or confess guilt; alternatives to institutional care are available.

Article 41
Supremacy of Higher Standards
The standards contained in this Convention not to supersede higher standards contained in national law or other international instruments.

APPENDIX 4

EXCERPTS FROM PL.104.193, THE PERSONAL RESPONSIBILITY AND WORK OPPORTUNITY RECONCILIATION ACT

Authors' note: This statement of purpose in the legislation is telling in its dismay about the 'crisis' of perceived increase in births to single mothers and in its insistence that 'entitlements' (human rights?) are hereby eliminated. It is also the clearest declaration that work and marriage are the solutions to poverty.

"(e) PENALTIES AGAINST INDIVIDUALS.

"(1) IN GENERAL.–Except as provided in paragraph (2), if an individual in a family receiving assistance under the State program funded under this part refuses to engage in work required in accordance with this section, the State shall–

"(A) reduce the amount of assistance otherwise payable to the family pro rata (or more, at the option of the State) with respect to any period during a month in which the individual so refuses; or

"(B) terminate such assistance, subject to such good cause and other exceptions as the State may establish.

Authors' note: This is the authorization to impose sanctions on families who fail to find or sustain work.

The exceptions identified below are controversial, since they rely on judgement of administrators concerning 'demonstrated inability to find childcare.'

"(2) EXCEPTION–Notwithstanding paragraph (1), a State may not reduce or terminate assistance under the State program funded under this part based on a refusal of an individual to work if the individual is a single custodial parent caring for a child who has not attained 6 years of age, and the individual proves that the individual has a demonstrated inability (as determined by the State) to obtain needed child care, for 1 or more of the following reasons:

"(A) Unavailability of appropriate child care within a reasonable distance from the individual's home or work site.

"(B) Unavailability or unsuitability of informal child care by a relative or under other arrangements.
"(C) Unavailability of appropriate and affordable formal child care arrangements.

Authors' note: the most punitive elements of the act are considered by many to be the 5 year limit on benefits:–

"(7) NO ASSISTANCE FOR MORE THAN 5 YEARS.–
"(A) IN GENERAL.–A State to which a grant is made under section 403 shall not use any part of the grant to provide assistance to a family that includes an adult who has received assistance under any State program funded under this part attributable to funds provided by the Federal Government, for 60 months (whether or not consecutive) after the date the State program funded under this part commences, subject to this paragraph.

Author's note: each state must submit detailed evidence of need as in 1994 and detailed planning before federal funds can be 'drawn down'. As a result, individual states vary widely in the percentage of federal funds they can acquire.

"PART A-BLOCK GRANTS TO STATES FOR TEMPORARY ASSISTANCE FOR NEEDY FAMILIES

"SEC.401.PURPOSE.

"(a) IN GENERAL.–The purpose of this part is to increase the flexibility of States in operating a program designed to–
"(1) provide assistance to needy families so that children may be cared for in their own homes or in the homes of relatives;
"(2) end the dependence of needy parents on government benefits by promoting job preparation, work, and marriage;
"(3) prevent and reduce the incidence of out-of-wedlock pregnancies and establish annual numerical goals for preventing and reducing the incidence of these pregnancies; and

"(4) encourage the formation and maintenance of two-parent
     families
"(b) No INDIVIDUAL ENTITLEMENT.–This part shall not be interpreted
     entitle any individual or family to assistance under any State
     program funded under this part.

"SEC.402.ELIGIBLE STATES; STATE PLAN.

"(a) IN GENERAL.–As used in this part, the term 'eligible State' means,
     with respect to a fiscal year, a State that, during the 2-year period
     immediately preceding the fiscal year, has submitted to the
     Secretary a plan that the Secretary has found includes the
     following:
     "(1) OUTLINE OF FAMILY ASSISTANCE PROGRAM.–
          "(A) GENERAL PROVISIONS.–A written document that
          outlines how the State intends to do the following:
               "(i) Conduct a program, designed to serve all political
               subdivisions in the State (not necessarily in a
               uniform manner), that provides assistance to
               needy families with (or expecting) children and
               provides parents with job preparation, work, and
               support services to enable them to leave the
               program and become self-sufficient.
               "(ii) Require a parent or caretaker receiving assistance
               under the program to engage in work (as defined
               by the State) once the State determines the parent
               or caretaker is ready to engage in work, or once
               the parent or caretaker has received assistance
               under the program for 24 months (whether or
               not consecutive), whichever is earlier.
               "(iii)Ensure that parents and caretakers receiving
               assistance under the program engage in work
               activities in accordance with section 407.
               "(iv) Take such reasonable steps as the State deems
               necessary to restrict the use and disclosure of
               information about individuals and families
               receiving assistance under the program
               attributable to funds provided by the Federal
               Government.
               "(v) Establish goals and take action to prevent and

reduce the incidence of out-of-wedlock pregnancies, with special emphasis on teenage pregnancies, and establish numerical goals for reducing the illegitimacy shall not be considered to be an expenditure under this part.

"(A) EXCEPTION RELATING TO TITTLE XX PROGRAMS.– All amounts paid to a State under this part that are used to carry out State programs pursuant to title XX shall be used only for programs and services to children or their families whose income is less than 200 percent of the income official poverty line (as defined by the Office of Management and Budget, and annually in accordance with section 673(2) of the Omnibus Budget Reconciliation Act of 1981) applicable to a family of the size involved.

"(e) AUTHORITY TO RESERVE CERTAIN AMOUNTS FOR ASSISTANCE.–A State may reserve amounts paid to the State under this part for any fiscal year for the purpose of providing, without fiscal year limitation, assistance under the State program funded under this part.

"(f) AUTHORITY TO OPERATE EMPLOYMENT PLACEMENT PROGRAM.– A State to which a grant is made under section 403 may use the grant to make payments (or provide job placement vouchers) to State-approved public and private job placement agencies that provide employment placement services to individuals who receive assistance under the State program funded under this part.

"(g) IMPLEMENTATION OF ELECTRONIC BENEFIT TRANSFER SYSTEM.– A State to which a grant is made under section 403 is encouraged to implement an electronic benefit transfer system for providing assistance under the State program funded under this part, and may use the grant for such purpose.

"(h) USE OF FUNDS FOR INDIVIDUAL DEVELOPMENT ACCOUNTS.–

"(1) IN GENERAL.–A State to which a grant is made under section 403 may use the grant to carry out a program to fund individual development accounts (as defined in paragraph (2)) established by individuals eligible for assistance under the State program funded under this part.

"(2) INDIVIDUAL DEVELOPMENT ACCOUNTS.–

"(A) ESTABLISHMENT.–Under a State program carried out under paragraph (1), an individual development account may be established by or on behalf of an individual eligible for assistance under the State program operated under this part for the purpose of enabling the individual to accumulate funds for a qualified purpose described in subparagraph (B).

"(B) QUALIFIED PURPOSE.—A qualified purpose described in this subparagraph is 1 or more of the following, as provided by the qualified entity providing assistance to the individual under this subsection:

"(i) POSTSECONDARY EDUCATIONAL EXPENSES.— Postsecondary educational expenses paid from an individual development account directly to an eligible educational institution.

"(ii) FIRST HOME PURCHASE.—Qualified acquisition costs with respect to a qualified principal residence for a qualified first-time homebuyer, if paid from an individual development account directly to the persons to whom the amounts are due.

"SEC.405.ADMINISTRATIVE PROVISIONS.

"(a) QUARTERLY.—The Secretary shall pay each grant payable to a State under section 403 in quarterly installments, subject to this section.

"(b) NOTIFICATION.—Not later than 3 months before the payment of any such quarterly installment to a State, the Secretary shall notify the State of the amount of any reduction determined under section 412(a)(1)(B) with respect to the State.

"(c) COMPUTATION AND CERTIFICATION OF PAYMENTS TO STATES.—

"(1) COMPUTATION.—The Secretary shall estimate the amount to be paid to each eligible State for each each quarter under this part, such estimate to be based on a report filed by the State containing an estimate by the State of the total sum to be expended by the State in the quarter under the State program funded under this part and such other information as the Secretary may find necessary.

"(2) CERTIFICATION.—The Secretary of Health and Human Services shall certify to the Secretary of the Treasury the amount estimated under paragraph (1) with respect to a State, reduced or increased to the extend of any overpayment or underpayment which the Secretary of Health and Human Services determines was made under this part to the State for any prior quarter and with respect to which adjustment has not been made under this paragraph.

"(d) PAYMENT METHOD.–Upon receipt of a certification under subsection (c)(2) with respect to a State, the Secretary of the Treasury shall, through the Fiscal Services of the Department of the Treasury and before audit or settlement by the General Accounting Office, pay to the State, at the time or times fixed by the Secretary of Health and Human Services, the amount so certified.

WORK ACTIVITIES

"(d) WORK ACTIVITIES DEFINED.–As used in this section, the term 'work activities' means–

"(1) unsubsidized employment;

"(2) subsidized private sector employment;

"(3) subsidized public sector employment;

"(4) work experience (including work associated with the refurbishing of publicly assisted housing) if sufficient private sector employment is not available;

"(5) on-the-job training;

"(6) job search and job readiness assistance;

"(7) community service programs;

"(8) vocational educational training (not to exceed 12 months with respect to any individual);

"(9) job skills training directly related to employment;

"(10) education directly related to employment, in the case of a recipient who has not received a high school diploma or a certificate of high school equivalency;

"(11) satisfactory attendance at secondary school or in a course of study leading to a certificate of general equivalence, in the case of a recipient who has not completed secondary school or received such certificate; and

"(12) the provision of child care services to an individual who is participating in a community service program.

"(e) PENALTIES AGAINST INDIVIDUALS.–

"(1) IN GENERAL.–Except as provided in paragraph (2), if an individual in a family receiving assistance under the State program funded under this part refuses to engage in work required in accordance with this section, the State shall–

"(A) reduce the amount of assistance otherwise payable to the family pro rata (or more, at the option of the State) with respect to any period during a month in which the individual so refuses; or

"(B) terminate such assistance, subject to such good cause and other exceptions as the State may establish.

"(2) EXCEPTION.–Notwithstanding paragraph (1), a State may not reduce or terminate assistance under the State program funded under this part based on a refusal of an individual to work if the individual is a single custodial parent caring for a child who has not attained 6 years of age, and the individual proves that the individual has a demonstrated inability (as determined by the State) to obtain needed child care, for 1 or more of the following reasons:

"(A) Unavailability of appropriate child care within a reasonable distance from the individual's home or work site.

"(B) Unavailability or unsuitability of informal child care by a relative or under other arrangements.

"(C) Unavailability of appropriate and affordable formal child care arrangements.

"(f) NONDISPLACEMENT IN WORK ACTIVITIES.–

"(1) IN GENERAL.–Subject to paragraph (2), an adult in a family receiving assistance under a State program funded under this part attributable to funds provided by the Federal Government may fill a vacant employment position in order to engage in a work activity described in subsection (d).

"(2) NO FILLING OF CERTAIN VACANCIES.–No adult in a work activity described in subsection (d) which is funded, in whole or in part, by funds provided by the Federal Government shall be employed or assigned–

"(A) when any other individual is on layoff from the same or any substantially equivalent job; or

"(B) if the employer has terminated the employment of any regular employee or otherwise caused an involuntary reduction of its workforce in order to fill the vacancy so created with an adult described in paragraph (1).

"(3) GRIEVANCE PROCEDURE.–A State with a program funded under this part shall establish and maintain a grievance procedure for resolving complaints of alleged violations of paragraph (2).

"(4) NO PREEMPTION.–Nothing in this subsection shall preempt or supersede any provision of State or local law that provides greater protection for employees from displacement.

"(g) SENSE OF THE CONGRESS.–It is the sense of the Congress that in complying with this section, each State that operates a program funded under this part is encouraged to assign the highest priority to requiring adults in 2-parent families and adults in single-parent families that include older preschool or school-age children to be engaged in work activities.

"(h) SENSE OF THE CONGRESS THAT STATES SHOULD IMPOSE CERTAIN REQUIREMENTS ON NONCUSTODIAL, NONSUPPORTING MINOR PARENTS.–It is the sense of the Congress that the States should require noncustodial, nonsupporting, parents who have not attained 18 years of age to fulfill community work obligations and attend appropriate parenting or money management classes after school.

"(i) REVIEW OF IMPLEMENTATION OF STATE WORK PROGRAMS.– During fiscal year 1999, the Committee on Ways and Means of the House of Representatives and the Committee on Finance of the Senate shall hold hearings and engage in other appropriate activities to review the implementation of this section by the States, and shall invite the Governors of the States to testify before them regarding such implementations. Based on such hearings, such Committees may introduce such legislation as may be appropriate to remedy any problems with the State programs operated pursuant to this section.

"SEC.408.PROHIBITIONS; REQUIREMENTS.

"(a) IN GENERAL.–

"(1) NO ASSISTANCE FOR FAMILIES WITHOUT A MINOR CHILD.–A State to which a grant is made under section 403 shall not use any part of the grant to provide assistance to a family–

"(A) unless the family includes–

"(i) a minor child who resides with a custodial parent or other adult caretaker relative of the child; or

"(ii) a pregnant individual; and

"(B) if the family includes an adult who has received assistance under any State program funded under this part attributable to funds provided by the Federal Government, for 60 months (whether or not consecutive) after the date the State program funded under this part commences (unless and exception described in subparagraph (B), (C), or (D) of paragraph (7) applies).

"(2) REDUCTION OR ELIMINATION OF ASSISTANCE FOR NON-COOPERATION IN ESTABLISHING PATERNITY OR OBTAINING CHILD SUPPORT.–If the agency responsible for administering the State plan approved under part D determines that an individual is not cooperating with the State in establishing paternity or in establishing, modifying, or enforcing a support order with respect to a child of the individual, and the individual does not qualify for any good cause or other exception established by the State pursuant to section 454(29), then the State–

"(A) shall deduct from the assistance that would otherwise be provided to the family of the individual under the State program funded under this part an amount equal to not less than 25 percent of the amount of such assistance; and

"(B) may deny the family any assistance under the State program.

"(3) NO ASSISTANCE FOR FAMILIES NOT ASSIGNING CERTAIN SUPPORT RIGHTS TO THE STATE.–

"(A) IN GENERAL.–A State to which a grant is made under section 403 shall require, as a condition of providing assistance to a family under the State program funded under this part, that a member of the family assign to the State any rights the family member may have (on behalf of the family member or any other person for whom the family member has applied for or is receiving such assistance) to support from any other person, not exceeding the total amount of assistance so provided to the family, which accrue (or have accrued) before the date the family leaves the program, which assignment, on and after the date the family leaves the program, shall not apply with respect to any support (other than support collected pursuant to section 464) which accrued before the family received such assistance and which the State has not collected by–

"(i) September 30, 2000, if the assignment is executed on or after October 1, 1997, and before October 1, 2000; or

"(ii) the date the family leaves the program, if the assignment is executed on or after October 1, 2000.

"(B) LIMITATION.–A State to which a grant is made under section 403 shall not require, as a condition of providing assistance to any family under the State program funded under this part, that a member of the family assign to the State any rights to support described in subparagraph (A) which accrue after the date the family leaves the program.

"(4) NO ASSISTANCE FOR TEENAGE PARENTS WHO DO NOT ATTEND HIGH SCHOOL OR OTHER EQUIVALENT TRAINING PROGRAM.–A State to which a grant is made under section 403 shall not use any part of the grant to provide assistance to an individual who has not attained 18 years of age, is not married, has a minor child at least 12 weeks of age in his or her care, and has not successfully completed a high-school education (or its equivalent). if the individual does not participate in–

"(A) educational activities directed toward the attained of a high school diploma or its equivalent; or

"(B) an alternative educational or training program that has been approved by the State.

"(5) NO ASSISTANCE FOR TEENAGE PARENTS NOT LIVING IN ADULT-SUPERVISED SETTINGS.–

"(A) IN GENERAL.–

"(i) REQUIREMENT.–Except as provided in subparagraph (B), a State to which a grant is made under section 403 shall not use any part of the grant to provide assistance to an individual described in clause (ii) of this subparagraph if the individual and the minor child referred to in clause (ii)(II) do not reside in a place of residence maintained by a parent, legal guardian, or other adult relative of the individual as such parent's, guardian's, or adult relative's own home.

"(ii) INDIVIDUAL DESCRIBED.–For purposes of clause (i), an individual described in this clause is an individual who–

"(I)   has not attained 18 years of age; and

"(II) is not married, and has a minor child in his or her care.

"(B) EXCEPTION.–

"(i) PROVISION OF, OR ASSISTANCE IN LOCATING, ADULT-SUPERVISED LIVING AGREEMENT.–In the case of an individual who is described in clause (ii), the State agency referred to in section 402(a)(4) shall provide, or assist the individual in locating, a second chance home, maternity home, or other appropriate adult-supervised supportive living arrangement, taking into consideration the needs and concerns of the individual, unless the State agency determines that the individual's current living arrangement is appropriate, and thereafter shall require that the individual and the minor child referred to in subparagraph (A)(ii)(II) reside in such living arrangement as a condition of the continued receipt of assistance under the State program funded under this part attributable to funds provided by the Federal Government (or in an alternative appropriate arrangement, should circumstances change and the current arrangement cease to be appropriate).

"(ii) INDIVIDUAL DESCRIBED.–For purposes of clause (i), an individual is described in this clause if the individual is described in subparagraph (A)(ii), and–

"(I)   the individual has no parent, legal guardian, or other appropriate adult relative described in subclause (II) of his or her own who is living or whose whereabouts are know;

"(II) no living parent, legal guardian, or other appropriate adult relative, who would otherwise meet applicable State criteria to act as the individual's legal guardian, of such individual allows the individual to live in the home of such parent, guardian, or relative;

"(III) the State agency determines that—

"(aa) the individual or the minor child referred too in subparagraph (A)(ii)(II) is being or has been subjected to serious physical or emotional harm, sexual abuse, or exploitation in the residence of the individual's own parent or legal guardian; or

"(bb) substantial evidence exists of an act or failure to act that presents an imminent or serious harm if the individual and the minor child lived in the same residence with the individual's own parent or legal guardian; or

"(IV) the State agency otherwise determines that it is in the best interest of the minor child to waive the requirement of subparagraph (A) with respect to the individual or the minor child.

"(iii) SECOND-CHANCE HOME.—For purposes of this subparagraph, the term 'second-chance home' means an entity that provides individuals described in clause (ii) with a supportive and supervised living arrangement in which such individuals are required to learn parenting skills, including child development, family budgeting, health and nutrition, and other skills to promote their long-term economic independence and the well-being of their children.

"(6) NO MEDICAL SERVICES.—

"(A) IN GENERAL.—A State to which a grant is made under section 403 shall not use any part of the grant to provide medical services.

"(B) EXCEPTION FOR PREPREGNANCY FAMILY PLANNING SERVICES.—As used in subparagraph (A), the term 'medical services' does not include prepregnancy family planning services.

"(7) NO ASSISTANCE FOR MORE THEN 5 YEARS.—

"(A) IN GENERAL.–A State to which a grant is made under section 403 shall not use any part of the grant to provide assistance to a family that includes an adult who has received assistance under any State program funded under this part attributable to funds provided by the Federal Government, for 60 months (whether or not consecutive) after the date the State program funded under this part commences, subject to this paragraph.

"(B) MINOR CHILD EXCEPTION.–In determining the number of months for which for which an individual who is a parent or pregnant has received assistance under the State program funded under this part, the State shall disregard any month for which such assistance was provided with respect to the individual and during which the individual was–

"(i) a minor child; and

"(ii) not the head of a household or married to the head of a household.

"(C) HARDSHIP EXCEPTION.–

"(i) IN GENERAL.–The State may exempt a family from the application of subparagraph (A) by reason of hardship or if a family includes an individual who has been battered or subjected to extreme cruelty.

"(ii) LIMITATION.–The number of families with respect to which an exemption made by a State under clause (i) is in effect for a fiscal year shall not exceed 20 percent of the average monthly number of families to which assistance is provided under the State program funded under this part.

"(iii)BATTERED OR SUBJECT TO EXTREME CRUELTY DEFINED.–For purposes of clause (i), an individual has been battered or subjected to extreme cruelty if the individual has been subjected to–

"(I) physical acts that resulted in, or threatened to result in, physical injury to the individual;

"(II) sexual abuse;

"(III) sexual activity involving a dependent

child;

"(IV) being forced as the caretaker relative of a dependent child to engage in nonconsensual sexual acts or activities;

"(V) threats of, or attempts at, physical or sexual abuse;

"(VI) mental abuse; or

"(VII) neglect or deprivation of medical care.

"(D) DISREGARD OF MONTHS OF ASSISTANCE RECEIVED BY ADULT WHILE LIVING ON AN INDIAN RESERVATION OR UNEMPLOYMENT.—In determining the number of months for which an adult has received assistance under the State program funded under this part, the State shall disregard any month during which the adult lived on an Indian reservation or in an Alaskan Native village if, during the month—

"(i) at least 1,000 individuals were living on the reservation or in the village; and

"(ii) at least 50 percent of the adults living on the reservation or in the village were unemployed.

"(E) RULE OF INTERPRETATION.—Subparagraph (A) shall not be interrupted to require any State to provide assistance to any individual for any period of time under the State program funded under this part.

"(F) RULE OF INTERPRETATION.—This part shall not be interpreted to prohibit any State from expending State funds not originating with the Federal Government on benefits for children or families that have become ineligible for assistance under the State program funded under this part by reason of subparagraph (A).

Author's note: the Individual Responsibility Plans are unusual in Federal legislation in their detail and specific guidelines as to content and practice.

"(b) INDIVIDUAL RESPONSIBILITY PLANS.—

"(1) Assessment.—The State agency responsible for administering the State program funded under this part shall make an initial assessment of the skills, prior work experience, and employability of each recipient of assistance under the program who—

"(A) has attained 18 years of age; or

"(B) has not completed high school or obtained a certificate of high school equivalency, and is not attending secondary school.

"(2) CONTENTS OF PLANS.–

"(A) IN GENERAL.–On the basis of the assessment made under subsection (a) with respect to an individual, the State agency, in consultation with the individual, may develop an individual responsibility plan for the individual, which–

"(i) sets forth an employment goal for the individual and a plan for moving the individual immediately into private sector employment;

"(ii) sets forth the obligations of the individual, which may include a requirement that the individual attend school, maintain certain grades and attendance, keep school age children of the individual in school, immunize children, attend parenting and money management classes, or do other things that will help the individual become and remain employed in the private sector;

"(iii) to the greatest extend possible is designed to move the individual into whatever private sector employment the individual is capable of handling as quickly as possible, and to increase the responsibility and amount of work the individual is to handle over time;

"(iv) describes the services the States will provide the individual so that the individual will be able to obtain and keep employment in the private sector, and describe the job counselling and other services that will be provided by the State; and

"(v) may require the individual to undergo appropriate substance abuse treatment.

"(B) TIMING.–The State agency may comply with paragraph (1) with respect to an individual–

"(i) within 90 days (or, at the option of the State, 180 days) after the effective date of this part, in the case of an individual who, as of such effective date, is a recipient of aid under the State plan approved under part A (as in effect immediately before such effective date); or "(ii) within 30 days (or, at the option of the State, 90 days) after the individual is determined to be eligible for such assistance, in the case of any other individual.

"(3) PENALTY FOR NONCOMPLIANCE BY INDIVIDUAL.–In addition to any other penalties required under the State program funded under this part, the State may reduce, by such amount as the State considers appropriate, the amount of assistance otherwise payable under the State program to a family that includes an individual who fails without good cause to comply with an individual responsibility plan signed by the individual.

"(4) STATE DISCRETION.–The exercise of the authority of this subsection shall be within the sole discretion of the State.

"SEC. 413. RESEARCH, EVALUATIONS, AND NATIONAL STUDIES.

"(a) RESEARCH.–The Secretary shall conduct research on the benefits, effects, and costs of operating different State programs funded under this part, including time limits relating to eligibility for assistance. The research shall include studies on the effects of different programs and the operation of such programs on welfare dependency, illegitimacy, teen pregnancy, employment rates, child well-being, and any other area the Secretary deems appropriate. The Secretary shall also conduct research on the costs and benefits of State activities under section 409.

"(b) DEVELOPMENT AND EVALUATION OF INNOVATIVE APPROACHES TO REDUCING WELFARE DEPENDENCY AND INCREASING CHILD WELL-BEING.–

"(1) IN GENERAL.–The Secretary may assist States in developing, and shall evaluate, innovative approaches for reducing welfare dependency and increasing the well-being of minor children living at home with respect to recipients of assistance under programs funded under this part. The Secretary may provide funds for training and technical assistance to carry out the approaches developed pursuant to this paragraph.

"(2) EVALUATIONS.– In performing the evaluations under paragraph (1), the Secretary shall, to the maximum extend feasible, use random assignment as an evaluation methodology.

"(c) DISSEMINATION OF INFORMATION.—The Secretary shall develop innovative methods of disseminating information on any research, evaluation, and studies conducted under this section, including the facilitation of sharing information and best practices among States and localities through the use of computers and other technologies.

"(d) ANNUAL RANKING OF STATES AND REVIEW OF MOST AND LEAST SUCCESSFUL WORK PROGRAMS.—

    "(1) ANNUAL RANKING OF STATES.—The Secretary shall rank annually the States to which grants are paid under section 403 in the order of their success in placing recipients of assistance under the State program funded under this part into long-term private sector jobs, reducing the overall welfare case-load, and, when a practicable method for calculating this information becomes available, diverting individuals from formally applying to the State program and receiving assistance.

"(i) CHILD ON POVERTY RATES.—

    "(1) IN GENERAL.—Not later than 90 days after the date of the enactment of this part, and annually thereafter, the chief executive officer of each State shall submit to the Secretary a statement of the child poverty rate in the State as of such date of enactment or the date of the most recent prior statement under this paragraph.

    "(2) SUBMISSION OF CORRECTIVE ACTION PLAN.—Not later than 90 days after the date a State submits a statement under paragraph (1) which indicates that, as a result of the amendments made by section 103 of the Personal Responsibility and Work Opportunity Reconciliation Act of 1996, the child poverty rate of the State has increased by 5 percent or more since the most recent prior statement under paragraph (1), the State shall prepare and submit to the Secretary a corrective action plan in accordance with paragraph (3).

    "(3) CONTENTS OF PLAN.—A corrective action plan submitted under paragraph (2) shall outline the manner of which the State will reduce reduce the child poverty rate in the State.

The plan shall include a description of the actions to be taken by the State under such plan.

"(4) COMPLIANCE WITH PLAN.–A State that submits a corrective action that the Secretary has found contains the information required by this subsection shall implement the corrective action plan until the State determines that the child poverty rate in the State is less than the lowest child poverty rate on the basis of which the State was required to submit the corrective action plan.

"(5) METHODOLOGY.–The Secretary shall prescribe regulations establishing the methodology by which a State shall determine the child poverty rate in the State. The methodology shall take into account factors including the number of children who receive free or reduced-price lunches, the number of food stamp households, and the county-by-county estimates of children in poverty as determined by the Census Bureau.

"SEC. 414. STUDY BY THE CENSUS BUREAU.

"(a) IN GENERAL.–The Bureau of the Census shall continue to collect date on the 1992 and 1993 panels of the Survey of Income and Program Participation as necessary to obtain such information as will be enable interested persons to evaluate the impact of the amendments made by title I of the Personal Responsibility and Work Opportunity Reconciliation Act of 1996 on a random national sample of recipients of assistance under the State programs funded under this part and (as appropriate) other low-income families, and in doing so, shall pay particular attention to the issues of out-of-wedlock birth, welfare dependency, the beginning and end of welfare spells, and the causes of repeat welfare spells, and shall obtain information about the status of children participating in such panels.

"(b) APPROPRIATION.–Out of any money in the Treasury of the United States not otherwise appropriated, there are appropriated $10,000,000 for each of fiscal years 1996, 1997, 1998, 1999, 2000, 2001, and 2002 for payment to the Bureau of the Census to carry out subsection (a).

"SEC.415.WAIVERS

"(a) CONTINUATION OF WAIVERS.–
  "(1) WAIVERS IN EFFECT ON DATE OF ENACTMENT OF WELFARE REFORM.–
    "(A) IN GENERAL.–Except as provided in subparagraph (B), if any waiver granted to a State under Section 1115 of this Act or otherwise which relates to the provision of assistance under the State plan under this part (as in effect on September 30, 1996) is in effect as of the date of the enactment of the Personal Responsibility and Work Opportunity Reconciliation Act of 1996 the amendments made by the Personal Responsibility and Work Opportunity Act of 1996 (other than by section 103(c) of the Personal Responsibility and Work Opportunity Reconciliation Act of 1996) shall not apply with respect to the State before the expiration (determined without regard to any extensions) of the waiver to the extend such amendments are inconsistent with the waiver.
    "(B) FINANCING LIMITATION.–Notwithstanding any other provision of the law, beginning with fiscal year 1996, a State operating under a waiver described in subparagraph (A) shall be entitled to payment under section 403 for the fiscal year, in lieu of any other payment provided for in the waiver.
  "(2) WAIVERS GRANTED SUBSEQUENTLY.–
    "(A) IN GENERAL.–Except as provided in subparagraph (B), if any waiver granted to a State under section 1115 of this Act or otherwise which relates to the provision of assistance under a State plan under this part (as in effect on September 30, 1996) is submitted to the Secretary before the date of the enactment of the Personal Responsibility and Work Opportunity Reconciliation Act of 1996 and approved by the Secretary on or before July 1, 1997, and the State demonstrates to the satisfaction of the Secretary that the waiver will not result in Federal expenditures under the title IV of this Act (as in effect without regard to the amendments made by the Personal Responsibility and Work Opportunity Reconciliation

Act 1996) that are greater than would occur in the absence of the waiver, the amendments made by the Personal Responsibility and Work Opportunity Reconciliation Act of 1996 (other than by section 103(c) of the Personal Responsibility and Work

"(b) SPECIAL RULE RELATING TO EMERGENCY ADVANCE PAYMENTS.–
Section 1631(a)(4)(A) (42 U.S.C. 1383(a)(4)(A)) is amended–

"(1) by inserting "for the month following the date the application is filed" after "is presumptively eligible for such benefits'; and

"(2) by inserting, "which shall be repaid through proportionate reductions in such benefits over a period of not more than 6 months" before the semicolon.

"(c) CONFORMING AMENDMENTS.–

"(1) Section 1614(b) (42 U.S.C. 1382c(b)) is amended–

"(A) by striking "or request" and inserting "on the first day of the month following the date the application is filed, or, in any case in which either spouse requests"; and

"(B) by striking "application or"

"(2) Section 1631(g)(3) (42 U.S.C. 1382j(g)(3)) is amended by inserting "following the month" after "beginning with the month".

"(d) EFFECTIVE DATE.–

"(1) IN GENERAL.–The amendments made by this section shall apply to applications for benefits under title XVI of the Social Security Act filed on or after the date of the enacment of this Act, without regard to whether regulations have been issued to pimplement such amendments.

"(2) BENEFITS UNDER TITLE XVI.–For purposes of this subsection, the term "benefits under title XVI of the Social Security Act" includes supplementary payments pursuant to an agreement for Federal administration under section 1616(a) of the Social Security Act, and payments pursuant to an agreement entered into under section 212(b) of Public Law 93-66.

SUBTITLE B–BENEFITS FOR DISABLED CHILDREN

SEC.211.DEFINITION AND ELIGIBILITY RULES.

"(a) DEFINITION OF CHILDHOOD DISABILITY.–Section 1614(a)(3) (42 U.S.C. 1382c(a)(3)), as amended by section 105(b)(1) of the Contract with America Advancement Act 1996, is amended–
"(1) in subparagraph (A), by striking "An individual" and inserting "Except as provided in Subparagrph (C), an individual";
"(2) in subparagraph (A), by striking "(or, in the case of an individual under the age of 18, if he suffers from any medically determinable physical or mental impairment of comparable severity)";
"(3) by redesignating subparagraphs (C) through (I) as subparagraphs (D) through (J), respectively;
"(4) by inserting after subparagraph (B) the following new subparagraph;
"(C)(i) An individual under the age of 18 shall be considered disabled for the purposes of this title if that individual has a medically determinable physical or mental impairment, which results in marked and severe functional limitations, and which can be expected to result in death or which has lasted or can be expected to last for a continuous period of not less than 12 months.

TITLE IV–RESTRICTING WELFARE AND PUBLIC BENEFITS FOR ALIENS

SEC.400.STATEMENTS OF NATIONAL POLICY CONCERNING WELFARE AND IMMIGRATION

The congress makes the following statements concerning national policy with respect to welfare and immigration:
"(1) Self-sufficiency has been a basic principle of United States immigration law since this country's earliest immigration statutes.
"(2) It continues to be the immigration policy of the United States that–
"(A) aliens within the Nation's borders not depend on

public resources to meet their needs, but rather rely on their own capabilities and the resources of their families, their sponsors, and private organizations, and

"(B) the availability of public benefits not constitute an incentive for immigration to the United States.

"(3) Despite the principle of self-sufficiency, aliens have been applying for and receiving public benefits from Federal, State, and local governments at increasing rates.

"(4) Current eligibility rules for public assistance and unenforceable financial support agreements have proved wholly incapable of assuring that individual aliens not burden the public benefits system.

"(5) It is a compelling government interest to enact new rules for eligibility and sponsorship agreements in order to assure that aliens be self-reliant in accordance with national immigration policy.

"(6) It is a compelling government interest to remove the incentive for illegal immigration provided by the availability of public benefits.

"(7) With respect to the State authority to make determinations concerning the eligibility of qualified aliens for public benefits in this title, a State that chooses to follow the Federal classification in determining the eligibility of such aliens for public assistance shall be considered to have chosen the least restrictive means available for achieving the compelling governmental interest of assuring that aliens be self-reliant in accordance with national immigration policy.